To my courageous and loving mother, *Carmen,*

for all of her sacrifice and support even when,

at seven years old, I wanted to be a garbage truck driver.

To my grandmother,

Dolores (Mama Lola),

the strongest and most humble woman I've ever known.

To my high school coaches, *William Blood*

and *Dean Schneider,*

for collectively being the father I never had

and always reminding me that $1 + 1 = 2$.

E YOUR *relationships* DEVELOP YOUR *spirituality* TAKE CONTROL

th BELIEVE IN YOUR *dreams* NURTURE YOUR *relationships* DEVE

ituality TAKE CONTROL OF YOUR *health* BELIEVE IN YOUR *dreams*

elationships DEVELOP YOUR *spirituality* TAKE CONTROL OF YOUR *h*

IN YOUR *dreams* NURTURE YOUR *relationships* DEVELOP YOUR *spi*

y TAKE CONTROL OF YOUR *health* BELIEVE IN YOUR *dreams* NURTURE YOUR

ships DEVELOP YOUR *spirituality* TAKE CONTROL OF YOUR *health*

reams NURTURE YOUR *relationships* DEVELOP YOUR *spiritual*

L OF YOUR *health* BELIEVE IN YOUR *dreams* NURTURE YOUR *relation*

P YOUR *spirituality* TAKE CONTROL OF YOUR *health* BELIEVE IN YOUR *dr*

E YOUR *relationships* DEVELOP YOUR *spirituality* TAKE CONTRO

CONFIDENCE is QUEEN

E YOUR *relationships* DEVELOP YOUR *spirituality* TAKE CONTROL

lth BELIEVE IN YOUR *dreams* NURTURE YOUR *relationships* DEVE

rituality TAKE CONTROL OF YOUR *health* BELIEVE IN YOUR *dreams*

elationships DEVELOP YOUR *spirituality* TAKE CONTROL OF YOUR h

IN YOUR *dreams* NURTURE YOUR *relationships* DEVELOP YOUR *spi*

y TAKE CONTROL OF YOUR *health* BELIEVE IN YOUR *dreams* NURTURE YOUR

ships DEVELOP YOUR *spirituality* TAKE CONTROL OF YOUR *health*

reams NURTURE YOUR *relationships* DEVELOP YOUR *spiritual*

L OF YOUR *health* BELIEVE IN YOUR *dreams* NURTURE YOUR *relatior*

p YOUR *spirituality* TAKE CONTROL OF YOUR *health* BELIEVE IN YOUR d

RE YOUR *relationships* DEVELOP YOUR *spirituality* TAKE CONTROL

CONFIDENCE is QUEEN

THE **FOUR KEYS** TO ULTIMATE BEAUTY THROUGH POSITIVE THINKING

SUSIE CASTILLO

A CELEBRA BOOK

Celebra
Published by New American Library, a division of
Penguin Group (USA) Inc., 375 Hudson Street,
New York, New York 10014, USA
Penguin Group (Canada), 90 Eglinton Avenue East, Suite 700, Toronto,
Ontario M4P 2Y3, Canada (a division of Pearson Penguin Canada Inc.)
Penguin Books Ltd., 80 Strand, London WC2R 0RL, England
Penguin Ireland, 25 St. Stephen's Green, Dublin 2,
Ireland (a division of Penguin Books Ltd.)
Penguin Group (Australia), 250 Camberwell Road, Camberwell, Victoria 3124,
Australia (a division of Pearson Australia Group Pty. Ltd.)
Penguin Books India Pvt. Ltd., 11 Community Centre, Panchsheel Park,
New Delhi - 110 017, India
Penguin Group (NZ), 67 Apollo Drive, Rosedale, North Shore 0632,
New Zealand (a division of Pearson New Zealand Ltd.)
Penguin Books (South Africa) (Pty.) Ltd., 24 Sturdee Avenue,
Rosebank, Johannesburg 2196, South Africa

Penguin Books Ltd., Registered Offices:
80 Strand, London WC2R 0RL, England

First published by Celebra,
a division of Penguin Group (USA) Inc.

First Printing, July 2008
10 9 8 7 6 5 4 3 2 1

Copyright © Susie Castillo, 2008
All rights reserved

Gratefully acknowledgment is made for permission to reprint the following copyright material: Recipe for Green Lemonade from *The Raw Food Detox Diet* by Natalia Rose. Copyright © 2005 by Natalia Rose. Reprinted by permission of HarperCollins Publishers.

CELEBRA and logo are trademarks of Penguin Group (USA) Inc.

LIBRARY OF CONGRESS CATALOGING-IN-PUBLICATION DATA
Castillo, Susie.
  Confidence is queen: the four keys to ultimate beauty through positive thinking/Susie Castillo.
     p.   cm.
  ISBN 978-0-451-22462-0
  1. Optimism.   2. Success.   3. Castillo, Susie.   I. Title.

  BF698.35.O57C37   2008
  646.7—dc22   2008005267

Designed by Jennifer Ann Daddio
Set in Mrs. Eaves

Printed in the United States of America

PUBLISHER'S NOTE
The publisher does not have any control over and does not assume any responsibility for author or third-party Web sites or their content.
    The recipes contained in this book are to be followed exactly as written. The publisher is not responsible for your specific health or allergy needs that may require medical supervision. The publisher is not responsible for any adverse reactions to the recipes contained in this book.
    Accordingly nothing in this book is intended as an express or implied warranty of the suitability or fitness of any product, service or design. The reader wishing to use a product, service or design discussed in this book should first consult a specialist or professional to ensure suitability and fitness for the reader's particular lifestyle and environmental needs.

CONTENTS

E YOUR *relationships* DEVELOP YOUR *spirituality* TAKE CONTRO

lth BELIEVE IN YOUR *dreams* NURTURE YOUR *relationships* DEVE

ituality TAKE CONTROL OF YOUR *health* BELIEVE IN YOUR *dreams*

elationships DEVELOP YOUR *spirituality* TAKE CONTROL OF YOUR *h*

E IN YOUR *dreams* NURTURE YOUR *relationships* DEVELOP YOUR *spi*

y TAKE CONTROL OF YOUR *health* BELIEVE IN YOUR *dreams* NURTURE YOUR

ships DEVELOP YOUR *spirituality* TAKE CONTROL OF YOUR *health*

reams NURTURE YOUR *relationships* DEVELOP YOUR *spiritual*

L OF YOUR *health* BELIEVE IN YOUR *dreams* NURTURE YOUR *relation*

P YOUR *spirituality* TAKE CONTROL OF YOUR *health* BELIEVE IN YOUR *d*

RE YOUR *relationships* DEVELOP YOUR *spirituality* TAKE CONTR

My adorable little Chihuahua, Lupe, and me visiting
my family in Massachusetts during the holidays.

YOUR *relationships* DEVELOP YOUR *spirituality* TAKE CONTROL

th BELIEVE IN YOUR *dreams* NURTURE YOUR *relationships* DEVE

ituality TAKE CONTROL OF YOUR *health* BELIEVE IN YOUR *dreams*

elationships DEVELOP YOUR *spirituality* TAKE CONTROL OF YOUR *h*

IN YOUR *dreams* NURTURE YOUR *relationships* DEVELOP YOUR *spi*

TAKE CONTROL OF YOUR *health* BELIEVE IN YOUR *dreams* NURTURE YOUR *r*

ships DEVELOP YOUR *spirituality* TAKE CONTROL OF YOUR *health* B

reams NURTURE YOUR *relationships* DEVELOP YOUR *spiritual*

L OF YOUR *health* BELIEVE IN YOUR *dreams* NURTURE YOUR *relation*

YOUR *spirituality* TAKE CONTROL OF YOUR *health* BELIEVE IN YOUR *dr*

E YOUR *relationships* DEVELOP YOUR *spirituality* TAKE CONTRO

We all have times when it seems like nothing's going our way—when it seems like everything we want is out of reach. Ever have those days when you'd rather stay in bed buried under your covers rather than face the world?

Me, too. Believe me—I've been there.

If you had asked me when I was a kid if I ever thought I'd be a beauty queen, I would have said, "No Way!" In my wildest dreams I never thought I'd enter—and then win!—a beauty pageant. Of course, like most little girls, I watched them on TV, but they seemed more like game shows to me—something to watch, but not actually *do.*

But I *did* do it. In 2003 I won the title of Miss USA. And even though I wasn't the most traditionally beautiful contestant, I think what made me stand out—and ultimately win—was my confidence. What made me change my mind about pageants? I realized that it was a great way to bring me closer to my goal of working in the entertainment industry. I always believed a girl like me *could* win one of those pageants. When I say "a girl like me," I don't mean I thought I was unattractive. I never felt I was inferior to the other girls in any way. But I knew I was very different from the typical beauty pageant girl. In those days, most girls who won pageants were ultrafeminine Caucasian girlie girls with straight hair, who came from rich families and were really into makeup and clothes.

I am so *not* any of those things. I'm more of a jock than a girlie girl. My hair is supercurly. I ran track and played volleyball. My family was far from wealthy. And I'm Latina. On top of that, I had no idea how to pick out the right jewelry, put on makeup, or style my hair for a pageant. My usual morning routine involved tying my hair back into a ponytail and throwing on a pair of sweatpants before running out the door for school (hoping to make it to first period on time)!

Winning Miss USA confirmed what I had come to believe long before that point in my life: even though society may value a certain standard of beauty (like those blond-haired, blue-eyed, superthin model types you see on TV and in magazines), that doesn't mean it's the *only* standard of beauty. Being beautiful and discovering true beauty comes from the inside out. It's about you discovering what's beautiful about you, knowing the right tools to enhance your beauty, and then emanating it.

So how did I go from Susie the jock to Glamour Girl? First, let me start at the beginning and tell you a little bit about where I came from.

I grew up in Methuen, Massachusetts, which is about thirty miles north of Boston. I lived with my mom and two sisters in a part of town that you could say was "on the wrong side of the tracks." It wasn't a hard-core ghetto, but there were certainly gangs, violence, and plenty of drug dealing happening right on my street. When I got into middle and high school, several of my friends went down the wrong path, joining gangs, drinking and doing drugs. A few even got pregnant by the time we got to sophomore year!

My homelife was also pretty intense. My father was either totally abusive toward us or totally absent from our lives. He was never interested in playing with us or helping us with homework or doing the normal things Dads do. He stayed out at the local sports bar playing dominos until two a.m., stumbling home drunk with lipstick on his collar from women who weren't my mother. Obviously, he was cheating. When he *was* home, he "disciplined" us, hitting my sisters and me with his belt, which often left welts on our thighs where it struck. We were all afraid of him and what he might do next.

Once I was playing hide-and-go-seek with the neighborhood kids—a bunch of girls *and boys*. My dad freaked out and yelled for me to come into the house. Once I was inside, he gripped me by the shoulders—hard—and said, *"Las ninas no juegan con ninos! . . . Little girls don't play with boys!"* I remember looking at him in confusion, thinking, "In school we all play together. How is this different?" But I couldn't tell him that—I was too afraid of how he'd react. I was sent to my room for the rest of the day for being "bad." Thinking back about that now, I get really angry because I was just being a normal kid and wasn't being "bad" at all.

Another time, I remember waking up to the sound of my parents yelling. I was hoping maybe I was having a nightmare, but—nope—it was all too real. I slowly opened the bedroom door a crack and peered into the living room. My mom was red in the face, crying, and asking Dad where he'd been all night. My father grabbed my mom's throat and shook her to the ground, trying to get her to be quiet. It was awful. All she wanted was for her husband to stop cheating on her and come home at a decent hour to be with his family. Dad stomped out of our apartment that night, leaving my mom crying in a heap on the living room floor. I ran out of my bedroom to see if I could help her. She had me call the police to report my dad because her English was poor. So there I was, a five-year-old girl on the phone with the Methuen police station trying to explain what my dad had done.

Even though my childhood was less than ideal, all the stuff that happened to me made me a really strong person. I knew I wanted more from life than what I saw around me. And even though my dad wasn't around, I felt lucky that my mom and grandmother were. They were my pillars—my biggest fans, always supporting everything I wanted to do. They also taught me self-discipline, how to set boundaries, and the importance of *trying* to accomplish things, even though they might seem impossible. It was through their example that I created four keys that have helped me get through good times and tough times by *relying on myself*.

My grandmother taught me how to stay true to my principles in the face of peer, media, or even family pressures. She grew up very poor in Puerto Rico and had to learn to trust her own instincts. She trained me to trust mine. My mother taught me how to create strong bonds with friends and family so I'd always have a support system of people to turn to, no matter how difficult my situation might be. After my father left, my mom brought my grandmother to live with us, and we were surrounded by aunts, uncles, and cousins, whom my sisters and I could go to at any time.

My mother's resilience in the face of my father abandoning our family showed me that even if certain parts of my life weren't perfect, I had the power to control my destiny. She took two—and sometimes three—jobs to support us. Because of her, I knew anything I wanted to accomplish, whether it was taking charge of my own health or setting goals and achieving success, was possible.

I always thought that someday I'd write a book, but I wasn't sure exactly what I would write about. I knew I wanted to tell my story and encourage other young women to take control of their lives and follow their dreams, just like I did. But it wasn't until 2003, when I won Miss USA, that I looked back over my life and thought, "Wow! How did I do this? How did I get here?" I had accomplished every giant goal that I ever set in my life—yet I knew there was still much more for me to accomplish. I realized how amazing my achievements were and started to consider what led me to this success.

Part of my job as Miss USA required going to public-speaking engagements, so I often spoke at high schools, conventions, and other events. Often I'd speak to troubled kids from my own neighborhood. That was always very rewarding because I could totally relate to what they were going through—I knew because I'd been there. Usually they had no idea that I had once been one of them, because I'd be onstage wearing the Miss USA sash and tiara. The kids were always shocked when I told them that I had graduated from the same schools they went to and lived in the same neighborhoods as they did. Most of them were Latinos, like me, so they beamed with pride when I told them that I was only the third Latina EVER to win Miss USA. I wanted them to know that if I could achieve my goals, they could do it, too. I loved sharing my story with them, hopefully inspiring them to try to achieve anything their hearts desired.

But soon I realized that becoming a model and winning Miss USA took a whole lot more than what I mentioned during the hour-long speeches I was giving. I began to think about what I really wanted to say to these kids and considered how

I could go about saying it. I realized the message I had to impart was about how I became a beautiful and successful woman through the power of positive thinking. I looked back over my life and discovered that I had created a prescriptive plan for myself that consisted of four specific parts: cultivating my spirituality, creating healthy relationships, taking charge of my image, and turning my dreams into reality. In fact, at first I didn't even realize I'd been following a set of guidelines, but now I recognize that I've been following them practically my whole life.

I think these guidelines came about through a combination of my mother's strong principles, which she instilled daily in my sisters and me, and my own internal desire to succeed. Looking back over my life, I began to analyze events in my life and characteristics of my personality. I had always done my best to be a good person and treat people with the respect we all deserve. That resulted in a deep caring for others and a true love for myself. I've always had great support from my family and always returned that love. I enjoyed fashion and tried to look my absolute best, even if I was wearing sweatpants! I've also been writing my goals down and posting them on my wall since I was fourteen years old. But like I said, it wasn't until I became Miss USA that I was able to look within myself and recognize that all those years something extraordinary had been guiding me. That's when I decided to write this book and tell my story, which is one of hope, inspiration, and truth.

I decided to call these guidelines "keys" because that's how I see them—as keys that can unlock your true strength and lead you on a path of self-discovery, empowerment, success, beauty, and ultimately, confidence. These keys are what helped me go from being a girl from Methuen, Massachusetts, to becoming Miss USA, an actor, a radio host, an

MTV VJ, a spokesperson for Neutrogena, and now a published author. They are my rules to live by and I want to share them with you. I hope they will inspire you to stay true to yourself and find success in whatever it is you choose to pursue.

THE *Four Keys*

TO UNLEASHING

YOUR ULTIMATE BEAUTY

#1 *Identify and Effectively Develop Your Spirituality*

It's imperative to have a strong sense of self. My first step in the journey toward confidence and true beauty was getting to know who I was and what I was made of. I call this "spirituality." Without a strong sense of spirituality, I wouldn't have been able to achieve my goals.

I first realized the true importance of spirituality when I was in high school and became a member of our school's Peer Leadership Group. The group had a pretty impressive role in our community—we encouraged local elementary school kids to stay in school, stay off drugs, and be responsible people. As a peer leader, my job was to be an inspirational role model. By performing funny plays about being loyal, loving, dedicated, respectful, and hardworking, our goal was to instill positive character traits in our young audience, who would hopefully, in turn, inspire those around them to make positive improvements in themselves and their community.

I always felt so good about myself on those days when we performed for the kids. On those evenings in particular, while brushing my teeth before bed, I'd catch a glimpse of myself in the mirror and I truly loved the person I saw staring back at me. I thought, "Here's the face of a person who cares for others, someone who's a leader, someone who isn't perfect, but is happy and confident." I felt like the most beautiful girl in the world.

What I learned from being part of that program is that having a strong spiritual center gave me more confidence than just about any-thing. I wasn't looking at my hair or my skin or my cheekbones when I was looking at myself in the mirror—I was looking at ME. The real me, the inner me—the giving, loving, radiant me.

#2 Embrace and Nurture Your Relationships

Everyone needs to develop a support system. Family and com-munity were (and still are!) really important to me. My dad might not have been around, but I was able to create my own cadre of reliable people I could call on.

Talk about a support system—I had twelve aunts and uncles and about fifty cousins on my mom's side—all the family one could ever need or want! Some of them lived close by, within walking distance, so my cousins were my best friends. If someone was ever in need, family was there to give what they could to help out. That's how it always was.

Still, it was my immediate family—my mom and sisters—that I was closest to. Mami always made us feel like we came first—that every-thing she did was done with us in mind. I think part of the reason I want to succeed in life is because, in a way, it's like paying my mom back for all her sacrifice and hard work. I couldn't have gotten to where I am today without her, and I think she wouldn't have been able to withstand my father leaving her if it hadn't been for us and the need to make sure we were fed, clothed, and loved.

#3 Take Control of Your Health and Body Image

Your body image is a reflection of your self-control and self-love. Winning Miss USA taught me that beauty comes from the inside out. Sure, I learned a lot of tricks along the way for looking good (which I'll share with you here!), but the most important thing I learned is that if I'm beautiful internally, I'm beautiful externally, as well. There's so much more to looking good than wearing the right lip gloss (although M·A·C's Viva Glam is my fave!).

Looking good starts with having a healthy attitude toward nutrition and exercise. When I decided to give modeling a shot, I wanted to appear as physically fit and healthy as I could. I wanted to achieve that from the inside out, so I started by altering my diet. I added more fresh fruits and vegetables to my diet, drank more water and natural juices, and then I began to include strength training in my workout routine. Within just a few weeks, I felt like a new person. I had more energy, a more positive outlook, and on top of that, because I felt so great, I really looked good, too.

That's when I realized that it was *me* who had the power to change not only my internal self, but also my physical appearance. I learned that *I* am the one who can make the biggest difference in the image I present to the world. Once I felt healthy on the inside I began to concentrate on my outward appearance. I learned how to wear makeup, do my hair, and choose the right outfit for my body. Altogether these things made a big difference both in how I looked and how I felt about myself. I had all the proof I needed that I was on the right track when, a year later, I signed with a modeling agency.

#4 *Believe in Your Dreams and Make Them a Reality*

Having long- and short-term goals keeps you positive, focused, and strong. My dreams and aspirations kept me moving forward, rather than letting me become discouraged by the poverty, drug use, and seemingly hopeless environment around me.

Thinking back over my life, I'd have to say there were several things that inspired the formation of Key #4. First, I believe seeing my mom make it all on her own was probably the single most inspiring aspect of my upbringing. Mami raised three daughters, had more than one job when necessary, made rent every month, got dinner on the table every night, and was there to make sure my sisters and I got plenty of motherly love. Watching Mami accomplish it all instilled in me a sense that I could make any dream come to fruition as long as I had plenty of determination and worked hard enough.

I was also lucky to have a couple of mentors in my life—my high school indoor track coaches, who encouraged me to do my best, not only in sports, but in every part of my life. They took on my triumphs as if they were their own and were always pushing me to do better and try harder, along with imploring me never to give up and always look toward the future.

The encouragement from those who loved me gave me the strength to recognize that I wanted more from life than what the neighborhood I grew up in offered. All those negative influences, like drug dealers, gang members, and poverty, actually encouraged me to succeed, because I wanted a life that didn't exist where we lived.

Finally, achieving one goal helped me realize I could achieve more goals, which made me realize that it was okay to attempt to make bigger and loftier dreams come true. Each accomplishment I had led to another one and then another one, from landing that first modeling contract to the moment where I really knew I'd made it—being crowned Miss USA.

The combination of my life experience is what has contributed to the development of these four keys. It's difficult to pinpoint any one thing that's singularly responsible for their development. I have to give credit to all of the people and events in my life because they've all influenced the keys in some way.

These four keys helped me develop what I call "true beauty." True beauty isn't about how you look—it's about so much more than that. True beauty starts from the inside. It's the part of you that is loving, giving, positive, and contented.

You've probably seen people with true beauty—they exude radiance, like the sun, and shine with self-esteem and a positive attitude. They also have the ability to make those around them feel good about themselves with an ease that seems to come naturally. Overall, what they possess is confidence. Confidence is what equals true beauty. It may seem like these self-possessed beauties were born with that attitude, but I can tell you they probably weren't. Having a strong sense of confidence takes practice—plus, most important, you need the right tools. And that's what I want to pass on to you: the tools that shaped who I am today.

Throughout my life, the four keys have helped me transform from a young girl unsure about her place in the world, wondering whether or not she fit in, to a woman who knows exactly who she is, what she wants, and that she has the power within her to do anything. I've found that, while this trans-formation to true beauty was my end goal, I couldn't be in this place without taking the small steps that led me here. You've heard that saying about how it's the journey that re-ally matters? I think that's true. The path I took to become Miss USA was just as rewarding as the night I got crowned. Following these keys will send you on your own journey of self-discovery—one on which you'll discover who you really are and how much power you have within you to achieve what's important to you. I'm certain that if you follow these four keys, you'll find—just like I did—your own confidence, your own "true beauty."

Whether or not you want to be a beauty queen, whatever your hopes, dreams, and aspirations are, I believe these keys can guide you toward finding your own beauty. They can help you achieve any goal you set out to accomplish—from getting into a great college, to becoming a successful CEO, to being a good friend, wife, and mother. You can use these keys to help you create a personal belief system, to be-come more positive, to give back, to tighten family bonds, to make (and keep!) friends, to get healthy (inside and out), to make your dreams come true—to become a content, confi-dent, truly beautiful you.

And once you've attained that, you can really do anything you put your mind to. Somehow when we're confident and positive, all kinds of possibilities and opportunities present themselves to us. It's like the law of attraction: depending on how we present ourselves to the world, we can attract positive or negative things to our lives.

You know bling, designer clothes, a fancy car—none of those things shows off the inner you, which is the most beautiful part of you. Believe me, I've met some of the world's most famous celebrities, who have all the right clothes and may appear to be beautiful on the outside, but deep down, some of them are the ugliest people I've ever been around. By knowing who you are and believing that you can achieve your goals—despite your family situation, how you look, where you live, and what people say—you can show your beauty to the world.

This book will guide you through the four keys and show you step by step how to employ them in your own life. Within each section I reveal the tips and tools that helped me master each key. I also share with you my personal experiences and tell you exactly how I implemented those tools in particular situations to become a more confident, in-control, and beautiful person, so you can see firsthand how and why the keys work. I've also included some exercises and recipes that will make using the keys in your everyday life, not only simple, but fun, too.

The keys are organized in such a way that you will be able to start practicing them right away. Once you start to follow them, I'm sure you'll see a big difference in yourself almost immediately. Each key builds upon the next one, so be sure to start with the first section, in which I show how to develop your spirituality. After you've learned how to feed your soul, you'll move onto the next key where you'll find out how to nurture the relationships with the important people in your life, whether it's your family or your friends. Next, I tell you about the beauty secrets that helped me win Miss USA, led to my being named one of the most beautiful by *People en Español*, and keep me looking my best each and every day. Finally, I reveal how you can turn your dreams into tangible, actual real-life accomplishments, just like I did.

If you follow these keys, I guarantee you will transform your life and become the beautiful, confident and successful person you've always dreamed of being. Use this book like a guide to your new self, and refer to it whenever you need encouragement, a pick-me-up, or advice from your long-lost sister—me! Remember that I'm here for you as you begin the journey into your new way of living, thinking and relating to the world and to yourself.

I'm writing this book because I want to share with you what worked for me. I know if the four keys could transform me, they can transform you, too. Here's why the four keys work: because they're all about you. Based on your life, your experience, what you need and what you want. I know they work because I followed them to help me become Miss USA, and I follow them to this day as my career continues to unfold.

Let's get started so you can start following them, too!

XOXO,
Susie

there *I was, standing onstage with dozens of* beautiful young girls, hoping to be Miss Teen USA 1998. I'd already won Miss Massachusetts Teen USA, so I thought I had a pretty good shot. My high heels were starting to pinch, and I had an itch on my back that was driving me crazy! My mouth was trembling from smiling for so long, and my hair had so much hairspray on it I could've used my head as a combat helmet. The music swelled and the announcer began to call out the finalists. I held my breath and squeezed the hand of the girl next to me. I closed my eyes, waiting for him to say, "And the next finalist competing for the title of Miss Teen USA 1998 is . . . Massachusetts!"

But he didn't say that. I didn't make runner-up, or third place, or even rank in the top fifteen! I was devastated. I had worked so hard, and during the two weeks of the pageant in Shreveport, Louisiana, many state directors and pageant fans had approached me saying that I looked great onstage and had a shot at the crown. "Get ready to hear your name called during the live show!" some said. Even Ali Landry, a former Miss USA and pageant commentator during the live telecast, said on air, "I'm surprised that Massachusetts didn't make it." Of course I cried—who wouldn't?

Then I realized I couldn't let this loss knock me off course. I still had the same goals, the same dreams, the same needs, wants, and desires. Losing Miss Teen USA actually made me more determined than ever. That failure gave me an unstoppable yearning for success. I decided to set a new goal, one that was even more challenging: Miss USA.

I knew that in order to reach that goal, I had to have a plan. So I refocused on the keys I had relied on through my life thus far and began applying them with even more fervor, step by step, on my journey toward becoming Miss USA.

In this section you'll be introduced to the first key, which is about identifying and effectively developing your spirituality. It's the first—and most important—step toward becoming the new you because it's all about discovering who you are. Uncovering your true self is an elemental part of the journey toward becoming your best self, the one that shines with confidence and beauty.

In order for me to complete the other three keys and become the successful person I am today, I had to start here. Key #1 put me on the right path for self-improvement and led me to become a more empowered, inspired, and independent person. I think of Key #1 as my own Declaration of Independence. You know that part in the Declaration that reads "we hold these truths to be self-evident"? I feel like Key #1 showed me how to make my personal truths self-evident. I realized that unless I know who I am, I'm not able to present my most authentic self to the world—the one that's guided by my own principles, beliefs, and truths. In this section I will guide you toward finding and nurturing your spiritual center, which will create a strong foundation from which you can build upon with the subsequent keys.

In Key #1, you'll learn how to get to know your true self by what I call "finding your groove." By that I mean you'll determine what's most important to you, what truths you believe in, how you view the world around you, how you view yourself, and how to stay true to those beliefs, even in the face of peer pressure, prejudice, or family drama.

You'll also get the scoop on how a positive attitude can change your life. Part of developing your spirituality requires maintaining an optimistic outlook on life—even in the face of difficult situations, like unhealthy family relationships, negative living environments, dealing with racism or sexism, or any trying circumstance you might experience. In this section I share with you the tools I use when I need to remain positive.

One of those tools involves changing your perception. For instance, being thankful for the good things you have in your life rather than dwelling on the negative things. I also reveal how I learned to appreciate the little stuff as well as the big stuff and why celebrating gratitude is essential to staying positive.

Key #1 will also teach you how to put the damper on your own negative thoughts. In order to maintain a positive spirit, you've got to tell your inner voice to zip it when it goes into critic mode. We all have those times when we think to ourselves, "I'm not smart enough. I'm not pretty enough. I'm not good enough." I will show you how to nix that negativity. I also share with you a trick I use for halting my own inner critic by replacing negative thoughts with a positive inner monologue or mantra. I will give examples of mantras that work for me and encourage you to use mine or find your own.

Next, I reveal to you how I turned my life around. Even though I grew up in a less-than-ideal situation I was able to become a successful, confident person. I give you tips on how I did it and how you, too, can rise above your circumstances no matter what your background. I show that it's not only possible, but in some cases, imperative in making the difference in your life to overcome whatever obstacles you might face.

They say that home is where the heart is. I've found that to be absolutely true. Now that I live three thousand miles from home, sometimes I just need to feel that homey vibe. I teach you how to create "home" wherever you are, whether it's a dorm room or a hotel room.

Then Key #1 will help you discover your passion. Everyone has a purpose in life. This section asks you to investigate what drives you, excites you, and makes you feel most empowered. Identifying your unique calling is a major step toward understanding and embracing your best self.

Finally, I reveal the single most important element of developing your spirituality—*giving*. I offer ideas on ways you can give by volunteering for a variety of causes and/or organizations. Plus, you'll learn the secret about giving—that it actually gives the giver as much as the receiver.

Key #1

IDENTIFY AND EFFECTIVELY
DEVELOP YOUR *Spirituality*

A perfect New England fall day. Mami and I
on my wedding day.

E YOUR *relationships* DEVELOP YOUR *spirituality* TAKE CONTRO

lth BELIEVE IN YOUR *dreams* NURTURE YOUR *relationships* DEV

ituality TAKE CONTROL OF YOUR *health* BELIEVE IN YOUR *dreams*

elationships DEVELOP YOUR *spirituality* TAKE CONTROL OF YOUR h

E IN YOUR *dreams* NURTURE YOUR *relationships* DEVELOP YOUR *spi*

y TAKE CONTROL OF YOUR *health* BELIEVE IN YOUR *dreams* NURTURE YOUR

nships DEVELOP YOUR *spirituality* TAKE CONTROL OF YOUR *health*

reams NURTURE YOUR *relationships* DEVELOP YOUR *spiritua*

L OF YOUR *health* BELIEVE IN YOUR *dreams* NURTURE YOUR *relatio*

P YOUR *spirituality* TAKE CONTROL OF YOUR *health* BELIEVE IN YOUR d

E YOUR *relationships* DEVELOP YOUR *spirituality* TAKE CONTR

This key is the first because to me, it's of the utmost importance. When I use the word spirituality, I don't mean it in a religious sense. I'm not discounting religion by any means. Religion can be a beautiful thing—it can be a source of comfort and guidance, and it can certainly teach you right and wrong and to be a moral person. But when I say "spirituality," I'm talking about your inner self, your heart, your spirit, and your feelings about yourself.

So in this section we're going to look at how to identify and develop your spirituality. This key is the most important step in building confidence and true beauty, because it's all about building your inner strength, finding out who you are, and what makes you *you*.

What does that mean? Think of it this way.

Finding your spirituality means discovering:

- what makes you tick
- what gets you excited

- what makes you glow
- what makes you think
- what makes you feel good about yourself
- what makes you love
- what makes you happy
- what makes you beautiful

Spirituality is what makes you feel alive. It's the compass that guides your decisions and gives you a sense of peace, purpose, and a feeling of connection to the people and world around you. It brings meaning to our lives and sends us on quests for awareness.

Spirituality is totally personal and individual. I like to think of my spirituality as my inner candle—always burning inside me no matter what. Okay . . . that may sound a little silly, but it works for me. My inner candle keeps my spirits up when I'm feeling down. It gives me hope when it seems like there is none. It keeps me positive when things seem to be going wrong. It guides me to make the right choices. It keeps me true to being me.

Identifying and Developing Your Spirituality

When I was a little girl my grandmother—my *abuela*—used to take me to church with her. We weren't really any specific religion, so Mama Lola went to whatever church she thought seemed interesting. She used to tell me, "Susie, God doesn't care where you go." To me that also means it's what you *do* that matters, and what's in your heart that's most essential—the place where you'll find stillness will bring inner peace and balance.

Find Your Groove:
Who Are You?

Finding your groove is all about:

- knowing who you are
- believing in yourself
- staying true to your beliefs and goals
- being positive

If someone were to ask you what you believe in, would you know how to answer? What are your personal truths?

Sometimes dealing with a difficult or sad situation can make you a stronger person—like if a family member dies or your parents divorce. Or trying something you've never tried before, like white-water rafting or belly dancing classes, to challenge yourself. Or even trying and not doing as well as you thought you would, like not getting the job you really, really, really wanted. All of these events contribute to making you a stronger, tougher person. They contribute to the development of your spirit.

When I was a kid I used to watch a show called *Lifestyles of the Rich and Famous.* The show was about how rich people lived—they highlighted what they owned and how much items cost. I used to think to myself, "Someday I'm going to be rich like that and buy my mom a house where she can retire. I'm going to pay for my sisters' educations, and we're going to have all the things in the world that we want." It was a far cry from the environment I lived in, but that's what I hoped to someday be able to create for myself and for my family. Even then I knew that becoming rich was about more than money. I knew I had to develop a strong sense of self first. You see, your spirit is more important than you think. It's your most powerful resource. And the best part about your spirit is that it belongs solely and completely to you. Nobody can touch your spirit.

Staying Positive

One of the most important elements of developing your spirituality is being positive and maintaining an optimistic outlook. I know this can be really hard to do. Sometimes you don't get the promotion you aimed for, you don't get accepted to the college you applied to, or you have a fight with your significant other or best friend. Believe me, I know we all have our moments—I'm not always Miss Upbeat-Happy-Go-Lucky. Sometimes I've got to pull myself out of ruts, too. But I do have some handy tools for staying positive:

1. Be thankful for what you *do* have, rather than worrying about what you *don't* have.
2. Be able to laugh at yourself.
3. Silence your inner critic.
4. Talk about yourself in a positive way.
5. Don't take on other people's negativity.

Be Thankful: Have an Attitude of Gratitude

One of the most important things I learned when I was younger was to be thankful for what I *did* have rather than bemoan what I *didn't* have. I was definitely jealous sometimes of friends who had fathers—even my friends with divorced parents got to see their dads regularly. Mami told me, "You've got everything you need right here—you have a mom, two sisters, and Mama Lola. What more could you ask for?" So that became one of the sayings that got me through that time. "What more could I ask for?" I'd ask myself when I was feeling sad or really missing my dad. My situation could have been much worse.

Appreciate
THE SMALL STUFF—AND THE BIG STUFF

Another thing I learned was to appreciate what I had. I would start off by listing little things like:

> *I'm thankful I have socks.*
> *I'm thankful I can walk to school (there was a kid in my school who was paralyzed and in a wheelchair).*
> *I'm thankful Mami made rice and beans for dinner tonight!*

Then I'd move to my gratitude for bigger things like:

> *I'm thankful Mama Lola has come to live with us.*
> *I'm thankful Mami loves us so much.*
> *I'm thankful we have our own apartment when we might have been homeless and living in a shelter.*

Celebrating the things in your life that really matter is very important. Think about all the things you're thankful for. What are they? What are the big things you appreciate? What about the small things? What do you appreciate about your mom or dad or someone else in your family? What do you appreciate about your friends? What do you appreciate about yourself?

I like to think about the things I'm thankful for every morning before I start my day. Before I get out of bed, I go over all the things in my life that are special and important—and I give a little thought of thanks for them. Whether it's good health, your sweet (and cute!) boyfriend, your supportive family, wealth, the yummy meal you had for dinner . . . whatever it might be . . . there's always something that will make you feel fortunate. It's a great way to start your day because it immediately puts you in a positive mood so you always wake up "on the *right* side of the bed!" Taking time out for a personal acknowledgment makes me feel good—and actually look good, too. Being grateful helps radiate inner joy and true beauty.

You've Got to Be Willing to Laugh at Yourself

I can be a total dork. In fact, I love being a goofball and making people laugh. My sister and I used to dance for Mami and Mama Lola when they were cooking. Mami would be stirring beans for that night's dinner and listening to the local Latin radio station. I'd dramatically ballet leap into the middle of the kitchen floor and start doing the merengue or salsa. Then my sister would come in and start dancing with me in big exaggerated steps. Mami would roll her eyes at us and laugh. As I got older, I continued making up my own silly steps and would dance for my friends. In college my friends called me the Puerto Rican Irish Step Dancer . . . aka Lady of the Dance!

Another one of my charming laugh-at-myself abilities is to imitate movie characters—like Al Pacino in *Scarface* or Borat. Being able to act goofy and laugh at myself has helped me shake off a bad day, deal with a stressful situation, give me perspective or not take things quite so seriously.

TRY THIS

Put on one of your favorite songs—for me, that's usually "What You Waiting For?" by Gwen Stefani—then get up and start moving. Even if you're not a dancer you can jump up and down or shimmy your shoulders, shake your hips, step side to side, or even copy moves you've seen in music videos or your favorite musical. Dancing is a really great way to boost your mood and it's great exercise! So, let yourself be a total goofball.

Quiet Your Inner Critic

Sometimes we can be our own worst enemies. When I was preparing to compete for the Miss USA Pageant, it was really easy to start feeling insecure when I knew there were fifty other beautiful girls who all wanted the same thing: the crown. I started to question myself. "Am I good enough?" "Am I wearing the right dress?" "Am I pretty enough?" I decided what I needed to do to quiet my doubts was show off the part of me that was different from the other contestants. In my case it was being Latina.

Which was pretty ironic since when I was growing up being Latino wasn't exactly considered cool. American media often portray Latinos as on welfare, uneducated, unwed teen mothers, or involved with gangs, drugs, violence, and crime. I knew lots of people who shunned their Puerto Rican, Dominican, or Cuban backgrounds because they wanted to fit in and be like everyone else. They also did things like never speaking Spanish in public. I even had some friends whose parents never taught them how to speak Spanish at all because they wanted them to be more "American."

I remember telling Mami once, "We live in America, Mom, so you have to learn to speak English like everyone else!"

She snapped back, "You, Susie Castillo, are Puerto Rican and *you* have to learn to speak Spanish because it's your culture and part of who you are!"

She was a tough one, I tell ya! In our home we spoke Spanish and Spanish only. Even today I speak only Spanish with my mom even though we both speak English!

When I was a kid, Mami used to send me to Puerto Rico to spend summers with my aunts, uncles, and cousins. I lived just like they did, taking walks to *la plaza* to buy *pirraguas de fresa*, which was a yummy strawberry treat just like an Italian Ice, and eating mangos, *parchas* (passion fruit), and *quenepas*, which are little round green balls with a thin outer shell that you use your teeth to cut open. Then you can eat the sweet inside but you have to be careful because there's a pit in the middle. My aunt had two *quenepas* trees in her backyard, so we would climb the trees to pick them. We would also attend *Las Fiestas Patronales*, an annual festival of music, food, and carnival rides. I actually never saw any of Puerto Rico's famous white sand beaches because I never did anything touristy.

By sending me to Puerto Rico, my mom taught me that we should embrace our rich culture and use our background to succeed, instead of dwelling on the negative aspects of it—like they often do on the news. There are a lot of stereotypes about Latinos I've passionately tried to help erase over the years, especially when I was Miss USA.

When I was preparing for the pageant, I saw that all the girls I was competing with were just as beautiful, athletic, and smart as I was. Just like me, most were also models who eventually wanted to work in the entertainment industry. So I knew I needed to highlight what was unique and special about myself in order to stand out. I realized what was unique about me was a no-brainer—it was my culture!

After that realization every part of my competition strategy, from my dress to my hairstyle, reflected my roots. My evening gown had ruffles on the bottom, which is very Latin. I wore my hair naturally curly because I knew that the majority of the contestants would be wearing their hair straight. I also wore big hoop earrings because at the time Jennifer Lopez was always seen sporting the same earrings. That was just another bit of Latin flavor I added to my look.

And then—how's this for positive karma?—the 2003 Miss USA Pageant was held in San Antonio, Texas, which has a HUGE Latino population! Plus, there were salsa dancers dancing in the background during the swimsuit and evening gown competitions! I felt as though the pageant was designed for me to win.

You can't ignore the things that make you different from everyone else. Embrace them! For me, those characteristics were what made me win Miss USA and helped me achieve what I have in my life. You have to feel good about your own unique qualities.

When your inner critic starts acting up, the first thing to do is acknowledge that you're thinking negatively. Then change what you're saying to yourself. Turn the "I can't" into "Of course I can." I like to think about myself in the same way I'd think about my best friend. I would never think to tell my closest friend that she's not good enough, not smart enough, or not pretty enough—so why in the world would I want to tell myself those things?

One way I turn my inner critic into my inner cheerleader is by creating positive affirmations—or words of encouragement—that I tell myself regularly. Things like:

- I am beautiful.
- I will be rich someday.
- I am loving.
- I am a great person.
- I am going to lose those ten pounds to be healthy.
- I work hard.
- I deserve what I have.

I like to write these affirmations on Post-its and place them around my desk and near my computer—anywhere I'll see them every day.

Develop an Inner Monologue

Another way I stay positive is by creating an inner monologue—that's a term I learned in acting class. Some people may also call it a personal mantra. But basically, it's a short saying that you repeat to yourself regularly to keep focused. The thought is that by actually stating your wishes or needs, you can better make them a reality. I also like to say them out loud, which is like declaring to the world what I want.

Sometimes my inner monologue is about who I am and what I believe in, like any of the following examples:

Inner Peace Equals Outer Beauty
Love Is All You Need
Treat People the Way You Want to Be Treated
Home Is Where My Heart Is

But sometimes my inner monologue is about stuff I want. When I was in high school, I would say things to myself like:

Our volleyball team is going to win Friday's game.
I'm going to get an A on my government paper.
That guy in fifth period is going to ask me out.

Now my inner monologue sounds more like:

I'm going to blow their socks off at the audition!
They're going to say, "We need to work with this girl!"
This is exactly the right part for me.
I was born for this job.

It's best to keep your inner monologue short, so you can remember the words. Set aside a few minutes throughout the day to repeat this mantra to yourself about three to five times. When you say it over and over to yourself, it becomes kind of like a meditation. I like to practice my inner-monologue meditation every morning when I wake up and every night before I go to bed. But sometimes I do it in the car while I'm driving, or while I'm hanging out with friends at dinner. Repeating my mantra for the day helps remind me of what I value in life and what I want to achieve next.

YOU'RE *a 10*

When I was preparing for the pageant, I took a confidence-building seminar called "Eagle U." One of the exercises they had us do was to write the number 10 on our palms with our fingers. Then we were asked to smack our foreheads with our palms.

"See—you're a 10!" the instructor shouted.

He said from then on we should walk around like 10s—especially since the number was now "imprinted" right on our foreheads. That really helped me see myself differently. I walked taller. I held my head up higher. After all, I was a 10, and I wanted everyone to know it!

Positive Self-Talk

I'm always really conscious of how I talk about myself to others. Whether I'm talking to my mom or my best friend, I don't dwell on the negative. I tell them about all the positive things going on in my life—all the good things that happen rather than the bad. That's not to say I ignore the negative stuff. If something really serious is going on, I share it with them, but I try my best not to complain.

SWITCHEROO

I like to change my inner critic words to inner cheerleader words. You know, change the negative connotation to a positive one. For example: When I was competing in Miss USA, I would say to myself, "I'm not *nervous*. I'm *excited*."

Don't Take on Negativity

When I was competing for the Miss Massachusetts USA pageant—I invited my family to come to the show. My uncle balked at the idea, saying, "Why would I want to waste my money on tickets? You're not going to win." Here was a member of my own family who didn't believe in me! His rude comment could have crushed me. But I was able to call on my inner cheerleader and use my inner monologue to let his words slide right off my back. Just because he couldn't imagine himself achieving anything big didn't mean I had to take on his negative attitude. I was able to realize that his reality wasn't my reality—and never would be. I had confidence in myself and was able to say, "Well, when I win it will be your loss that you weren't there to see it!"

The main thing I want to emphasize—and I think the best advice I can give—is never to let other people's negativity affect you. Call on your mantra, and then go ahead and give your goal a TRY. It's one thing to say you're going to do something, but then you've got to actually try to do it. In the box to the right is one of my favorite sayings.

> *"You're only going to be as successful as the foot you put forward."*

KEEP *a Journal*

Writing in a journal can help you discover your inner voice. Take time every day to reflect on your day and what you want in life. You can write about whatever you want, but I find it easier to focus if I answer questions. For instance, you can start with these three:

What do you love about yourself?
What was the happiest moment of your day?
What do you really want in your life?

Turn It Around: Rise Above Your Circumstances

As I mentioned before, throughout my life I've had to deal with all kinds of people who have preconceived notions about who Susie Castillo is because I'm Latina—my mother was born in Puerto Rico and my father in the Dominican Republic. This happened most frequently when I was in high school. There was a guy who sat behind me in Spanish class who once said, "All Puerto Ricans do is come to America to go on welfare." Was he serious? His comment made me furious, and I couldn't keep quiet.

I shot back at him, "You know, my mom had to go on welfare because my dad took off. But she worked three jobs and was only on welfare a short time to get back on her feet!" The guy became sheepish and mumbly, and turned back to his Spanish book. But his words really touched a nerve in me. I remembered what it was like receiving free food from the government and going to the market with food stamps to buy groceries. It was a humbling experience to hand over those bills in order to get eggs and milk.

Then I dated a guy whose parents didn't approve of me, because his mother was worried I was going to end up pregnant and ruin her son's life. That was what she thought about Puerto Rican girls . . . that they were all pregnant teenagers! *Ay yai yai*, did that piss me off!

Both of these situations lit a fire under me, further fueling my desire to be successful and to break the American stereotypes of Latinos, and Puerto Ricans, in particular.

Unfortunately, some of the kids around me did start gravitating toward stereotypical behavior. People I'd known since elementary school started to join gangs and sell drugs. They thought that they had no alternative and that in our neighborhood it was just what you did. Because I knew who I was and because I had my inner candle guiding me, I always felt there was a different path for me. I knew that outside my neighborhood the world was full of opportunities for me. I just had to go for them.

You've probably experienced some situation in your life where someone made assumptions about who you are—based on where you live, who your parents are, your nationality, what you look like, what sports you play, what you like to read, how you dress, and on and on. Or maybe it was your own voice telling you *you're too this* or *not enough that*. But stereotypes, prejudices, and especially ignorant comments don't determine who you are. Your neighborhood, background, cultural heritage, and gender are certainly part of what makes up your character, but take me for example.

I'm not *just* Latina. I didn't *just* grow up on the worst street in Methuen, Massachusetts. I'm not *just* a girl. I'm much more than any of those single things. I'm a complex combination of those things and much, much more—just like you.

I could have looked at my life and said, "This sucks. I don't have a dad. We live in a bad neighborhood. My neighbor sells drugs. I'm just going to give up and sell drugs, too." But I didn't. I turned my situation around and so can you.

It doesn't matter whether your background is like mine or not. We all face times that are tough, when we want nothing more than to give up. But I want you to think about "turning it around." What could be considered a negative situation to some could actually inspire your desire to succeed, to set a goal, to stay focused, to try something you never thought you would.

In her book, *The Power of the Actor,* my acting coach, Ivana Chubbuck, says, "Overcoming and winning against all the hurdles and conflicts of life is what makes dynamic people. Martin Luther King, Jr., Stephen Hawking, Susan B. Anthony, Virginia Woolf, Albert Einstein, Beethoven, Mother Teresa and Nelson Mandela all had to overcome almost insurmountable struggles in their lives to achieve their goals. Indeed, the greater the obstacles and the more passion these people brought to overcoming their obstacles, the more profound the achievement or contribution they made. They didn't become amazing, accomplished people despite their challenges, but because of them."

You see, I believe that if I hadn't grown up in that bad neighborhood, if my dad hadn't left our family, if I didn't have to deal with ignorance and racism, I wouldn't be who I am today. So, believe it or not, I am actually grateful for all of the challenges in my life. They've shaped me into the woman I am today—a strong, courageous, beautiful, successful woman.

Home Sweet Home

Home is more than an address or a neighborhood or a house for me. Home is the place I feel most comfortable, the most like myself, the most loved, and the most welcome. It's also the place I can be with the people I love most. When I was a child we lived in a small three-bedroom apartment on the third floor. There were four of us living in that apartment—and for a while, when Mama Lola lived with us, there were five! I shared a room with my two sisters. But our apartment never felt small because there was always so much love in the house.

Every night at five o'clock, my sisters and I would rush through the back door of our apartment, through the line of laundry Mami had hanging in the back hallway to dry, into the kitchen. We were tired out from school and after-school playtime. The homey smell of rice and beans and fried *platanos maduros* filled the air. (*Platanos maduros*, sweet plantains, are a Puerto Rican specialty—they look like bananas and are totally yummy!) Dinner was ready, and Mami was always there to dish up heaping portions.

I think one of the reasons home was such a special place for me was that I really felt like it was mine. After my father left, we *all* had to help out a lot more by doing chores. I'm not saying I was thrilled to do them or anything—no way! Who likes scrubbing the bathroom floor on Saturday afternoon when all your friends get to go to the movies? But looking back, I definitely think that because all of us contributed to the household in our own way, we all felt like we were part of creating a **home**. I always had a sense of responsibility toward making our house nice and keeping it clean. That's one thing I remember: even though we didn't have expensive furniture or fancy decorations, our house was always neat and tidy. I'm thankful that Mami had so much pride in our home, because she passed that on to us, and now I'm very conscious of the way I care for my own house. You know, like that saying "*Mi casa es su casa*" (**"My house is your house"**)? I like to think of it as "**My house is our house**," because it belongs to all of us.

Creating Home

AWAY FROM HOME

When I was competing in beauty pageants (Miss Massachusetts USA, then Miss USA, and finally Miss Universe), I had to be away from home often. But I always brought a few things with me so no matter where I went, I had a little bit of home with me. The first thing I pack are photos—pictures of those people who are the most important to me. And I always bring *mi Lily*. I can't believe I'm telling you this, but when I was little I had a favorite blanket—you know, a blanky. It was one of those blankets with the silky edges. I called it *mi Lily*—or my Lily. I used to take it everywhere with me. Every time one *Lily* wore out, I'd get a new one. Even now when I travel, I take my Lily on the plane with me. I actually bought a baby blanket for myself to travel with! I roll it up and make a pillow or just wrap it around me to stay warm. It's really comforting and therapeutic.

Here's how you can create your own home away from home if you travel often: keep some of your favorite things that say home in a bag—like a backpack or travel bag—so you can take it with you. Maybe your favorite book or magazine, a scented candle that reminds you of the smell in your home, a CD with your favorite songs, pictures of your favorite times with family and friends. Maybe even your favorite stuffed animal from when you were a kid—or your blanky, like me! You get the idea. It's all about having that comforting feeling of home—no matter how far from home you are.

Food for Your Soul

Another way I create home away from home is by cooking. One of my favorite dishes to whip up is something that Mami always made when I was growing up: *platanos fritos*, or fried plantains. Plantains are kind of like bananas, but when they're fully ripe they're sweeter. Mami's recipe is really a side dish, but I love it so much that I eat the plantains alone sometimes. When I was a kid I used to eat them so often that my family called me "*come platano*," which was a funny way of teasing me. I still eat them and look forward to my visits with Mami so she can fry me up a plate to go along with her awesome *arroz con habichuelas* (rice and beans). Some of my friends like macaroni and cheese. Some go for sweets. Others want mashed potatoes. But *platanos fritos* are my comfort food. I could eat them every single day—they're that good. I don't really eat fried foods, so when I make them at home, I boil them and mash them up with butter, mashed potato–style. Each bite feeds my soul and makes me feel like I'm back in Massachusetts in Mami's kitchen. My favorite Mexican restaurant in Los Angeles, Frida, makes *platanos maduros* perfectly, so that's where I eat them fried. They're really easy to make and yummy, so I think you're going to love them as much as I do!

¡COME PLATANO! RECIPE

1 superripe plantain (The skin is dark like a rotting banana and mushy to the touch. It may seem rotten but it's actually just ripe and will be yummy. I promise!)

vegetable oil (enough so that it almost covers the plantain slices)

a medium-sized frying pan

a dinner plate layered with a couple of paper towels

ketchup (as much as you want)

1. Peel the plantain and cut the fruit in quarter-inch angled slices.

2. Pour oil in the pan and set on the stove over medium heat.

3. Carefully place the plantain slices in the oil, using a fork.

4. When the slices start to darken and turn a light brown color, take them out of the oil and place them on a paper towel–covered plate. The paper towel will soak up any excess oil.

5. Squeeze some ketchup on the side of the plate and enjoy!

6. Don't forget to turn the stove off! Yes, I've left it on before because I've been so excited to take a bite.

Find Your Passion

Knowing what you're passionate about—what makes you feel good and feeds your inspiration—is another step on the road to developing your spirituality.

I wasn't the best student in the world. In fact, I didn't really like school all that much. I knew it was important—college was definitely part of my plan—so I did my homework and wrote papers, but I never had a 4.0 or anything. What I did do, though, was find what I was passionate about in school.

And that turned out to be sports, being a peer leader, and being part of student government. I ran track and played volleyball, put on plays about self-esteem and staying on the straight and narrow for elementary school kids, and ran for student government. I was always a leader and liked to get involved.

I was also really into interior decorating. No joke. I used to rearrange all the furniture in our house at least once a month—and if my mom happened to pick out new curtains without me? Well, she'd get an earful: "Why didn't you take me with you? You know *I'm* the one who decorates our house!" I was also kind of the family event designer. My grandparents had many kids, so I had lots of cousins, which meant it was always somebody's birthday. I was the one who made sure the flowers on the cake matched the napkins and the tablecloths. I was the one who hung the balloons and streamers and laid everything out just right. Later, when I went to college and had to choose a major, it was a no-brainer: interior architecture and design.

My other big passion was modeling. I used to look at fashion magazines while we were in line at the supermarket, and wish I could be one of those glamorous girls in the magazine with the fabulous makeup and clothes. I started to wonder, "Could that be me?" I used to put on fashion shows for my family. I'd turn on my favorite tunes and strut down the long hallway of our apartment, practicing turns.

Cindy Crawford was my celebrity inspiration because even though she was so sophisticated, beautiful, and glamorous, she also seemed like a real person—just a normal girl like me. I once read in a magazine that one of her guilty pleasures was Cheez Whiz—you know, that cheese-in-a-jar stuff? I was psyched to find this out because Cheez Whiz was one of my favorite foods, too! Knowing this funny little detail made me feel a kinship with her that really inspired me.

So how do you find your passion?

Finding your personal passion might take a little time, but it's another step on the way to true beauty because being passionate can make you a happier and more fulfilled person. Start by thinking about what makes your heart sing. What do you get excited about? What do you and your friends discuss the most? What do you love to do more than anything else in the world?

Not everyone knows exactly what her passion is. And sometimes it changes over time. Maybe you'll be really into wanting to be a lawyer one year, and the next it'll be a journalist. That's okay. Being involved in lots of things that interest you is a great way to uncover your passion.

GET *Passionate*

Jot down answers to the following questions to see what you're passionate about:

1. What's important to you?
2. What's your favorite thing in the whole world to do?
3. What hobbies or extracurricular activities do you enjoy?
4. What's your favorite sport?
5. What do you enjoy reading?

6. What do you love to talk about?
7. If you could spend all your time doing one thing, what would it be?
8. What makes your heart sing?
9. What makes you feel good about yourself?
10. What makes you feel proud of yourself?

Try It On for Size

Once you have an idea of what your passion might be, give it a whirl. Have you always wanted to learn how to paint? Take an art class. Always wanted to be a dancer? Grab a pal and teach yourselves some moves. It's good to try different things. It's like taking your passion for a test drive. And you'll find that it's enjoyable to try new activities with a friend. It builds your passion and your support system.

The next step is turning your passion into reality. The fourth key is all about setting and realizing goals, but you should know what your passion is before you start setting goals.

Giving Equals Getting

I've found that one of the most rewarding ways to develop my spirituality is by giving. Both my mother and grandmother always encouraged my sisters and me to help other people. Mama Lola would always tell us, "No matter how little you have, there is always someone out there who has a lot less than you." Regardless of what we had or didn't have, they said we could always find a way we could give *something*.

My grandmother and mother were both humble women who grew up *en el barrio* (a very poor neighborhood) in Juana Diaz, a town on the small island of Puerto Rico. Mami remembers her family never went without a meal, but they ate meat only once a week because it was so expensive. For breakfast they ate buttered bread with a cup of coffee. For lunch it was *guanemos y arenca*—a doughy potato dish, like gnocchi—with a side of cod, and water. They never had juice or soda. They didn't even have a refrigerator until Mami was ten years old. Clothes were a whole other story. They wore shoes in shifts! One of my aunts would go to school in the morning, and when she got home, she'd pass her shoes on to her sister, who went to school in the afternoon!

As they grew up, the oldest kids moved to the United States to make money, which they sent home to the family. When Mami and Mama Lola told these stories, it helped me realize how lucky I was to have the life I had.

Just up the street from us in Methuen lived a little girl who rode the bus with me to school. She was beautiful, with shiny blond hair and a cherubic face, but her clothes were always old, worn, and dirty. She was such a nice and well-behaved girl—always very polite and sweet. I wished someone could help her and see that she was well cared for.

One day I rushed home from the bus stop and ran to the window in our apartment to watch her walk by. Normally when I got home from school, I'd give my mom a big hug hello and say *bendicion*, which means "blessings"—it's the traditional way Puerto Rican children greet their parents and relatives. But this time I went straight to the window.

"Did you forget about the *bendicion*?" my mom asked me.

Then she noticed that I was crying. When she asked what was wrong, I told her all about the little girl and how I wished someone could help her.

"Why don't *we* help her? We could give her some of *our* things, couldn't we?" Mami suggested.

We put together a box of clothes and toys and took them to the little girl's house. When she saw all the "new" (well, new to her) things, she was so happy her face glowed, making her look even more like an angel. Seeing her gratitude filled me with intense joy. This was when the importance of giving really hit home for me. Even though we didn't have a lot of money, we could still make a difference in someone's life.

In high school, I started organizing and participating in neighborhood cleanups. We lived in an urban area, so often there was trash on the sidewalks. I organized the neighbors to get together once a year, and we'd hit the street, sweeping and picking up trash. What was great was that people would see us out there making our community a better place, and they'd grab their brooms and join us.

The most important thing I learned about giving was learning *what* I could give. Okay, so I wasn't a millionaire, but I did have some extra time, so I found a way to give by donating my skills. I was always great at organizing and cleaning up.

Giving develops your spirituality because it makes us feel good to help others. Sure, everyone likes to get presents, but giving is even more of a gift. It can bring so much to our spiritual selves. I also found that giving gives back—for instance, it gave me tons of self-esteem.

Think about what kinds of things you're good at or what you like to do.

Even if you're a teenager living at home you can do a lot.

Here are a couple examples of girls who took a small idea and turned it into something big.

Nora Ross was just three when she and her father passed a homeless man on the street in her neighborhood. She wanted to help him, but didn't know how she could. Later, she noticed a bowl filled with pennies at a neighbor's house and asked if she could give that change to the homeless man. The neighbor gave her the bowl. She then began to collect more pennies—her own, and others from kids at school—and now that small idea from a little girl has turned into a program called Common Cents, in which thousands of schools and kids participate and raise hundreds of thousands of dollars each year.

From that one little idea!

Another young woman, Kendall Ciesemier, started an organization called Kids Caring 4 Kids, which helps raise money for children in Africa who were orphaned when their parents died of AIDS. She set out to earn sixty thousand dollars and ended up earning a million!

What Can You Give?

Think about what you have to offer. How much free time do you have? What kinds of things are you interested in? What are you good at? Can you find a way to combine your passion and help the less fortunate? Answering these questions should help you discover what kind of volunteer work is right for you. Here are some suggestions that might be useful in your search.

If you like to read, think about becoming a tutor or reading stories to the elderly in a nursing home, or to kids at a day-care center. When I was in high school, my entire indoor track team, including our coaches, took a day off from practice to visit the local nursing home during the holidays. We would bring holiday cards and cookies and other holiday treats. Some of us even wore Santa hats to really get into the spirit. We found that what the patients loved most was when we sang Christmas carols. There were always a few of them who cried because they were so happy to have company.

There are some great literacy programs that offer volunteer opportunities through the following organizations:

ProLiteracy Worldwide: www.proliteracy.org
Sit Stay Read!: www.sitstayread.org
Reading Is Fundamental: www.rif.org

If you like talking on the phone, use that skill to volunteer for a crisis hotline. There are several suicide and other prevention hotlines in most major cities. Check out the National Suicide Prevention Lifeline Web site for more information (www.suicidepreventionlifeline.org) or help runaway youth through the National Runaway Switchboard (www.1800runaway.org).

If you like to cook, soup kitchens often need volunteers to serve meals to homeless people. Thanksgiving or other holidays are perfect occasions to give some of your time. Visit www.secondharvest.org to find out about soup kitchens in your area.

Do you like to work with your hands? You can volunteer for an organization like Habitat for Humanity, which helps build homes in poor or disaster-ridden areas. Or organize your own neighborhood cleanup like I did. Here's how I did it: I made some flyers and slipped them in all my neighbors' mailboxes. I also recruited my friends in the neighborhood. Cleanups inspire people to take pride in what might otherwise be a crummy neighborhood. My attitude was always "Just because it's the ghetto and there aren't any big houses on our street, it doesn't mean that we have to live with garbage." I also organized planting days. Every year on Earth Day, I'd get the neighbors together to plant flowers or trees. It was fun and a great way to do community service. Visit www.habitat.org to find out about building programs going on in your area.

If you're an animal lover, you might volunteer at your local animal shelter or rescue organization. The Society for the Prevention of Cruelty to Animals offers many volunteer opportunities. You can find out more on their Web site at www.spca.com.

If saving the environment is your cause, participate in programs to make your school or workplace more eco-friendly through the National Resources Defense Council Green Squad. Visit www.nrdc.org for more information. Also check out Earth Share at www.earthshare.org, the Sierra Club at www. sierraclub .org, and the Earthday Network at www.earthday.net.

You can also raise money for your favorite cause by having a yard sale, a bake sale, or a craft fair to benefit your favorite charity. You can help create your own charity event, or get involved in one, through an organization called On Your Feet Project. Find out more information on their Web site at http://www.oyfp.org. Also look into the American Red Cross—I'm a member of their celebrity cabinet—at redcross.org and UNICEF at www.unicef.org. These are outstanding organizations that have many ways for you to give.

There are so many ways you can give—you just have to know where to look. My favorite charities are the Hispanic Heritage Foundation and Voto Latino, which encourages Latinos to vote. There's also a wonderful organization called Sparrow Clubs (www.sparrowclubs.org) where you can raise money for a "sparrow" in your town or start a club in your school. It's great.

The simplest way to give is by treating people with dignity and respect. I live my life by the "golden rule": treat others how you would like to be treated.

Not sure what you want to do to help? Check out Volunteer Match at www.volunteermatch.org or USA Freedom Corps at www.freedomcorps.gov.

Giving GIVES YOU

- a sense of responsibility
- the lesson of sacrificing and giving more of yourself
- tolerance of others
- stronger friendships, family relationships, and community bonds, and a feeling of belonging
- inner beauty that shines—and leads to making your outer beauty glow

Spirituality Is Key

As you can see, identifying and effectively developing your spirituality is the most important key because knowing who you are empowers you, improves your self-esteem, and imbues you with confidence. It's the first step in developing your true inner beauty.

Remember...

IN ORDER TO IDENTIFY AND DEVELOP YOUR SPIRITUALITY, YOU MUST:

FIND YOUR GROOVE: Figure out who you are and what you believe in, and always stay true to yourself and your beliefs.

STAY POSITIVE: Keep an optimistic outlook.

BE THANKFUL: Have an attitude of gratitude.

LAUGH AT YOURSELF: Don't take things too seriously all the time.

QUIET YOUR INNER CRITIC: Stop self-criticism.

DEVELOP AN INNER MONOLOGUE: Create a personal mantra or positive affirmation and repeat it to yourself regularly.

POSITIVE SELF-TALK: Speak about yourself positively instead of dwelling on what you dislike about yourself.

DON'T TAKE ON NEGATIVITY: Keep others' negativity at bay—it's not about you; it's about them.

YOU CAN TURN IT AROUND: No matter what your family circumstances, you are more than where you come from.

FIND YOUR PASSION: Discover what excites you and chase it.

TAKE TIME-OUTS: Give yourself breaks now and then to revive your spirit.

GIVE TO GET: Help others to help yourself.

Now that you understand how to identify and develop your spirituality, you should be well equipped to begin the next phase of my four-part plan toward true beauty. Identifying and developing your spirituality will help you in all aspects of your life, from learning how to create healthy relationships, to being in charge of your own body image, to accomplishing your biggest goals.

You can apply the lessons presented in the first key to situations you deal with every day, whether it's learning how to remain optimistic even when you're having "one of those days" to quieting your inner critic when it rears its ugly, negative voice. I still use Key #1 all the time because I find that staying in tune with my spirituality keeps me balanced and focused—two essential frames of mind I definitely need to maintain as my career in Hollywood progresses!

I hope that you've recognized how essential it is to stand by your personal truths, beliefs, principles, and ideals. Following your inner compass and trusting your instincts will help you develop inner strength and, in turn, confidence.

As you continue reading this book and move forward in your journey toward unleashing your ultimate beauty, be sure to continue applying the concepts discussed in Key #1. As you start working on Key #2, which is all about nurturing your relationships, remember that the first—and most important—relationship is the one with yourself. You can't love others until you learn to love yourself.

RE YOUR *relationships* DEVELOP YOUR *spirituality* TAKE CONTR

lth BELIEVE IN YOUR *dreams* NURTURE YOUR *relationships* DEV

ituality TAKE CONTROL OF YOUR *health* BELIEVE IN YOUR *dreams*

relationships DEVELOP YOUR *spirituality* TAKE CONTROL OF YOUR *h*

E IN YOUR *dreams* NURTURE YOUR *relationships* DEVELOP YOUR *sp*

y TAKE CONTROL OF YOUR *health* BELIEVE IN YOUR *dreams* NURTURE YOUR

iships DEVELOP YOUR *spirituality* TAKE CONTROL OF YOUR *health*

lreams NURTURE YOUR *relationships* DEVELOP YOUR *spiritua*

)L OF YOUR *health* BELIEVE IN YOUR *dreams* NURTURE YOUR *relatio*

P YOUR *spirituality* TAKE CONTROL OF YOUR *health* BELIEVE IN YOUR *d*

RE YOUR *relationships* DEVELOP YOUR *spirituality* TAKE CONTR

one *day I came home from school to find Mami sitting* at the kitchen table, crying, her head buried in her hands. Lying next to her on the table was a letter from my father saying he was leaving us. On top of abandoning us, he had also taken all our money—he'd gone to the bank and withdrawn every last penny in our savings account. My mom was left with nothing. No money, no husband. Somehow Mami mustered all her strength, and vowed to keep our family together—with or without a father. To help out, Mama Lola moved in with us.

It was a difficult and sad time for all of us without him. Every night I cried into my pillow so nobody would hear me. I missed my dad and was scared about what might happen to us. But every morning the pain hurt a little less. Every day our small family became a little stronger. Whenever we felt gloomy about not having a father around, Mami would say to us, "You have me, you have Mama Lola. You have our family—that's all you need." She was right.

Mami became my rock, my biggest supporter. As a kid, I was obsessed with our garbageman. Seriously! Okay, well it was more the garbage *truck* than the garbage*man* that I was into. But I thought he was the luckiest guy in the world because he got to drive that truck! I loved watching the way the arms came down the sides of the truck, lifted the Dumpster up to unload the trash, and squished all that garbage into flat, tiny pieces. Awesome! I told Mami, "Someday, when I grow up, I want to be a garbage truck driver!" Without missing a beat, Mami said, "Of course, Susie—you can be anything you want to be."

That was how it always was in our house. Both Mami and Mama Lola were supportive no matter what we wanted to do. My goals became their goals, and they were going to help me reach mine no matter what. All of us took care of one another like that, becoming closer than we could have imagined. The result was a deepened love for one another, which really instilled in me the importance of nurturing healthy, strong relationships.

Our tight-knit bond definitely facilitated all my achievements, including winning Miss USA. Knowing I had a support system I could count on no matter what gave me courage, drive, and oodles of confidence. My family was there to cheer me on, or cheer me up, and to remind me never to give up on myself. That's a beautiful thing.

In Key #2 you'll learn how to create and cultivate positive relationships in your life and will discover why maintaining healthy relationships is so vital to my plan. I give you specific ways for nurturing and dealing with everyone in your life, from family and friends to significant others. My philosophy is that none of us can make it in this world all by ourselves, even though in our quest to be strong, independent women we often try to do everything ourselves. I show you that it's okay to ask for help. In fact, in order to become successful, you will probably have to ask for help at some point in your life. I know that without a support system, I never would have been able to go as far or accomplish as much in my life as I have.

This section imparts the wisdom I gained from my own *familia*. I pass on valuable techniques I learned for getting along with parents, siblings, and relatives. In addition, I relay stories about how my mom, sisters, and grandmother became a tight-knit unit, dependent upon one another's love, support, trust, and commitment. I show you examples of how respecting your parents and looking at issues from their perspective—even when you don't agree with their rules—are important steps toward becoming a mature adult. I also point out how and where you can find a mentor, should you need extra assistance or outside guidance to help with personal, spiritual, or career matters.

Next I instruct you on how to choose the right kind of friends and give examples of where you can meet people who are likely to share your same interests and values. For those on the shy side, I give examples of some simple conversation starters.

I also share with you pointers on what it takes to be a great friend and how to be there for one another in good times, as well as in bad. You can take a quiz to determine what kind of friend you are—the Cruise Director or the Comedian? I also offer fun, creative suggestions of things you can do to show your pal how much you appreciate her.

Relationships aren't always about love and gifts. Sometimes they can be downright difficult and even turn sour. Key #2 will show you how to stay away from people who aren't right for you, as well as how to set boundaries, speak your mind, and how to know when to walk away from a friendship.

I show you the right way—and the wrong way—to break up with a friend.

You'll also learn about dating in Key #2. Find out which kind of guy is right for you by completing a fun exercise that will help you narrow down the features you find most attractive in a potential mate. I list my dating dos and don'ts. And share my favorite day- or night-date activities—none of which will bust your wallet (or his!). I suggest ways to keep the lines of communication open and share tricks my husband and I practice all the time for maintaining a healthy and open relationship. Lastly, I offer my shoulder and give you tips on how to deal with the suckiness of heartbreak.

Key #2

EMBRACE AND NURTURE YOUR

Relationships

PHOTO BY MARISELE SIGMAN

My fantastic husband, Matt, and I.

YOUR *relationships* DEVELOP YOUR *spirituality* TAKE CONTRO

th BELIEVE IN YOUR *dreams* NURTURE YOUR *relationships* DEV

ituality TAKE CONTROL OF YOUR *health* BELIEVE IN YOUR *dreams*

elationships DEVELOP YOUR *spirituality* TAKE CONTROL OF YOUR *h*

IN YOUR *dreams* NURTURE YOUR *relationships* DEVELOP YOUR *spi*

y TAKE CONTROL OF YOUR *health* BELIEVE IN YOUR *dreams* NURTURE YOUR

ships DEVELOP YOUR *spirituality* TAKE CONTROL OF YOUR *health*

reams NURTURE YOUR *relationships* DEVELOP YOUR *spiritua*

L OF YOUR *health* BELIEVE IN YOUR *dreams* NURTURE YOUR *relatior*

P YOUR *spirituality* TAKE CONTROL OF YOUR *health* BELIEVE IN YOUR *d*

E YOUR *relationships* DEVELOP YOUR *spirituality* TAKE CONTR

The second key is embracing and nurturing your relationships because creating and maintaining positive relationships are essential to building self-esteem and confidence. Strong bonds with family and friends provide a support system of people who love you and will be there for you. It's like having a safety net, just in case you need one.

It Takes a Team

I like to think of a family as a team, *un equipo*. You're all there to support one another and work together. The family's common goal is to make life harmonious so you can go out into the world and be successful, happy, and fulfilled. That's definitely how it was—and still is—in my family. Mami, Mama Lola, my sisters, and I are extremely tight. We still rely on one another for advice, support, and encouragement—even though we don't all live together in the same apartment, or even the same state.

How to Deal with Family Relationships

As you become an adult and move on in your life—whether you go off to college or move into your own apartment—chances are, you're going to grow apart from your *familia*. This is normal. You're exploring your independence, having unique experiences, and meeting lots of new people. But it's important not to lose sight of who matters to you most. Remember that your family was your first support group, so it's important to maintain close-knit ties with them.

Siblings

There were times my sisters and I fought. Of course, it was always about the dumbest little things—you know, things you and your brothers and sisters have probably fought about, too. Most of the time my older sister reprimanded my little sister and me, as if she were our mother. Whenever she did this, I'd yell, "You're not my mother, so stop acting like it!" Which would inevitably cause an even bigger fight. Then we'd usually stomp away in opposite directions of the apartment, to vent for a while.

When I went away to college, my relationships with my sisters changed. We were no longer fighting over clothes, who didn't do their chores, or who spent too much time in the bathroom. All those petty annoyances became a thing of the past. Because we didn't live together anymore and weren't dealing with the day-to-day issues that can sometimes be difficult on relationships, we were able to get to know one another as individuals—as people rather than sisters. I think we've become even closer now that we're grown-ups. They're the first people I call (after Mami, of course!) when I have good news to share or need to discuss an important issue.

It took work to get to that point, though. It wasn't always easy. We still argue sometimes, but we handle it differently from the way we did when we were kids. Over the years I've learned that there are some essentials for nurturing positive relationships with siblings (though these elements work when dealing with other family members, friends, and boyfriends, too). The essential elements are respect, trust, and communication.

RESPECT

Every relationship requires respect, first and foremost. You've got to respect your sibling's feelings, thoughts, decisions, ideas, and sometimes even their space or privacy. It's imperative that you appreciate one another as you are, understanding and accepting both good and bad qualities, as well as abiding by personal boundaries. Hopefully they'll respect yours, too.

TRUST

Trust is another essential element of family relationships. You've got to be able to count on one another—for love, support, honesty, and commitment. Your family space is the one place where you should always feel safe. In order to create that safe haven, you need to foster a stable environment in which your siblings know they can count on you and vice versa. For example, when you say you're going to do something, do it. Don't give a bunch of empty promises and then never follow through. Also, try to be loyal, dependable, helpful, and positive toward your family members as often as possible. You and your siblings should be able to call on one another no matter what kind of situation might arise.

COMMUNICATION

You have to be able to talk to one another. Sharing your feelings with your siblings can bring you much closer together. By opening up and revealing vulnerabilities about one another, you can transform your relationship from childhood housemates to mature confidants. You should be able to talk to one another in a nonjudgmental way about just about anything. Sisters and brothers can provide great shoulders to lean on, and because they know you so well and know your history, they often have better advice than friends. Not to mention, because they're family and love you unconditionally, they usually always have your back.

Sometimes you might need to air a grievance with a sib, if they did something that hurt your feelings or crossed a boundary that made you feel upset or uncomfortable. You shouldn't bottle up those feelings—eventually they could pile up until you have a laundry list of things they did wrong (according to you) and either create undue stress for you or cause you to explode in anger at them—and to them it will seem like it's coming out of nowhere because you never let on that anything was wrong. The best thing to do if you need to have a confrontation is to sit your brother or sister down and tell them how what they did made you feel. You don't want to sound like you're blaming them for being a bad person; you want them to understand how their actions affected you.

Even more important than talking to your siblings is being able to *hear* them. Listening is very important when it comes to communication. One-sided conversations aren't very rewarding to either person. You should both share your thoughts and feelings, so allow time for them to speak up, too. When listening to their side, try to be understanding and really pay attention to what your sister or brother is telling you. Can you see the disagreement from their side?

If your discussion escalates into an argument, or you are prone to disagreements, it's imperative that you learn how to have a respectful disagreement. Yelling, name-calling or all-out brawling is totally unacceptable (even if when you were kids your fights evolved into wrestling matches, now that you're adults, fights should never become physical). When my sister and I have a disagreement, and we just can't see eye to eye, we take a break from each other in order to calm down and (hopefully) gain some perspective. Once we've cooled down, we come back together and resume our discussion, without anger. Then we try to really share our feelings and get to the root of the problem. I can't stress this enough: you have to be willing to open up, be vulnerable, and talk things out; otherwise you might have the same argument over and over again.

Here are some other ways to handle conflict with your brothers and sisters.

Choose your battles. Not everything should be an argument, but some issues are worth discussing. Think about what's really upsetting you and approach the conversation in a calm and rational way.

Consider your timing. If you know your bro is having a bad day, maybe it's not the right time to bring up how mad you are at him. He's already feeling bad enough. Don't kick him when he's down. Again, use patience and wait for a time that isn't so intense. The conversation will go better once enough time has passed for your emotions to calm down.

Let it go. Sometimes all you need to do is to step back, take a breath, and be a little more patient with your sibling. Sure she totally embarrassed you in front of your new boyfriend, but maybe she thought that story about you getting a bean stuck in your nose was endearing. Maybe she thought he would find it cute and make him even more into you. Or maybe your sister just has a big mouth, and you've gotta love her anyway. Sometimes backing off and not turning something into an argument is the right thing to do.

Nix the name-calling. My sisters and I used plenty of foul language on one another as teenagers. We could be relentless with the teasing and name-calling. But now that we're adults, we never use that kind of language. Calling names is both disrespectful and immature. Plus, it would be *muy* embarrassing for someone to see us act like that.

Talk to your parents if your conflict with your sibling spirals out of control or becomes confusing. You don't want to be a tattletale or try to get Mom or Dad on your side. What you should be trying to encourage is their insight about the situation. Mami can always give me the right kind of advice—and she knew plenty, having grown up with seventeen brothers and sisters!

Nurture your relationships. Just as important as knowing how to communicate with your siblings, you've also got to *nurture* your relationships with them. That means spending quality time together doing things like going to the movies, out for dinner, or taking spa days or weekend trips together. When my sister and I lived closer to each other, we'd often go shopping together at the mall. It was a fun way for us to bond. In that environment, we could be friends, as well as sisters. It also gave us a chance to talk about stuff that was bothering us—if we needed to—without arguing.

Parents

Sometimes it seems like Mom and Dad—in my case Mami—don't get us at all. I'll never forget the time when I was still in high school, and my mom and I got into a huge argument because she wouldn't let me go to a nine p.m. movie. Mami wanted me *home* by nine! My plan was to go to dinner with my friends and then a movie. She said, "Skip dinner and go to an earlier movie." I tried to explain to her that the rest of my friends' parents were cool with our plan, but she wouldn't hear it. It was her way or the highway. I argued with her that she was being completely unreasonable—which was a total no-no. To her, I was being disrespectful, which really ticked her off. One thing you definitely don't want to do is piss off a Latin mom! Needless to say, I didn't go *anywhere* that Saturday night. Instead of a fun movie with my friends, I was stuck at home watching *Sábado Gigante*—a variety show on Univision—with my mom!

It seemed like once I became a teenager my relationship with my mom changed. I wasn't a little girl anymore. I had new responsibilities, new friends—and I felt like I could and should be able to make my own decisions. Another thing that caused a lot of arguments was the fact that my mom grew up in a totally different country from me. I felt she wasn't "American enough" when it came to raising us. I was often pointing out she was much too strict and had to loosen up. I knew my friends had arguments with their parents. But at my house, we couldn't even look Mami in the face! In Puerto Rican culture it's considered rude. So, when she was talking to me, I had to keep my head down and never look up unless she asked me a question. Talk about strict, huh?!?

Once I went away to college, I could see that all those rules

I'd thought were unreasonable had actually prepared me for the discipline and hard work I needed for college, and for my career. I realized she set those limitations and boundaries because she loved me and wanted me to succeed. When I think about all those times I used to tell Mami to chill out with the rules, and she'd say, "You'll appreciate it when you're older. You'll get it," I feel like yelling, "Argh! Mami was right." Now I really do appreciate everything that she did for me.

The college I attended wasn't too far from home, so I could visit anytime I wanted and often stayed for weekends or weeknight dinners. Even though I was still close, the dynamic of my relationship with my mom changed. She was no longer in charge of my daily schedule—I was. She didn't set my curfew, or tell me who I could hang out with or where I could or couldn't go. But she was still my mom, and she still had her own ideas about what was right for me. So we had a period of adjustment getting used to our new roles. I found that if I just followed a few guidelines when dealing with Mami it helped a lot—these work whether you're dealing with your mom, dad, grandparents, stepparents, aunts, uncles, or guardians.

STAY IN TOUCH

You may find it helpful to check in with your family when you don't live at home. Of course your life is busy, but a simple phone call or e-mail will let your parents know you're okay, and that you're thinking of them and care.

GIVE THEM THE 411

Let your folks know what's going on in your life—whether you have a new friend or boyfriend, got a great job on campus, or have changed your major—again. You don't have to reveal every single detail, but give them some information about what you're up to. This will give them plenty of things to brag about to their friends!

BRING YOUR FRIENDS HOME

If you can, introduce your parents to your friends so they know the kind of people you're hanging out with. I always loved bringing my girlfriends over to Mami's for dinner, so they could get a nice home-cooked, tasty meal, and Mami would feel comfortable about whom I spent my time with.

STAY COOL

Every once in a while, you'll probably have a tiff with your parents. It happens. But you're not a kid anymore, and you need to deal with conflicts in a mature way. If you're feeling like you want to shout, take a deep breath and count to ten. Then try to resume talking to them as calmly as possible. You want them to take you seriously—not like a little kid having a tantrum. Think about what you say before you say it. Screaming like you did when you were twelve won't get you anywhere.

BE UNDERSTANDING

If you think moving out of the house is going to be hard for you, well, your leaving home is going to be just as hard on your parents. This period is a transitional phase for both of you. You're no longer their little kid, and it might take time for them to get used to you being a responsible young adult.

Moms and dads often get so used to their children being home and depending on them that they might experience a bit of depression when their children move out. This is called empty-nest syndrome. Your folks might call you more than they used to, or try to visit you often. Know that their reaction is likely temporary. As long as you keep in touch with them, let them know how you're doing, and give them a few details about your new life, they will likely eventually back off. They just love you and want to be assured that you are okay—so be patient.

Family Time

Even though you've got a whole new life, you've still got to make time for your family. Spending quality time with your family fosters bonding, creates stronger ties, and encourages deeper communication. Our family time was mostly spent in the kitchen. Both Mami and Mama Lola were great cooks, so all of us would gather in the kitchen and help cut up veggies, or stir the *arroz*. We'd have the Latin station on and all dance and cook together. Those times are seared in my memory. We could let our guard down and talk about our day, guys we thought were cute, or just about anything. Even today when we get together, we all seem to congregate in the kitchen and whip up some yummy dishes. If cooking's not your thing, there are plenty of ways to create family time—like taking hikes, going to the beach, going to the movies, or even just hanging out playing cards. All of these extra activities can make the times you spend together even more meaningful.

Find a Mentor

What happens if you don't have a parent to guide you? In my case, I didn't have a dad, and I really missed out on having a strong father figure—even though my mom was the best parent I could ever ask for. Still, I needed male guidance in my life. I was lucky; I found two mentors through my involvement in sports.

My coaches—Coach Schneider and Coach Blood—really kept me in line. They had all these goofy sayings, like "What's one plus one, Castillo?" to which, of course, I'd reply, "Two." Basically it meant that if I were going down the wrong path, doing drugs, getting too involved with boys, not doing well in school, "one plus one" wouldn't equal "two" anymore. It was their way of making sure I knew what was important. They encouraged me to focus on sports and my grades. They got me to keep my eye on the ball by looking toward the future, which they expected would be college and a good career.

I would highly recommend seeking a mentor. Look around your community—is there a teacher or coach who inspires and encourages you? Perhaps the adviser of one of the clubs you belong to? Or how about your boss, college counselor, or one of your professors? Having an authority figure you can consult when you're facing a difficult issue, or need career or personal advice, makes all the difference in the world. Knowing that my mentors were both there for me when I needed them helped lessen the pain I felt about my father. They also inspired me to work even harder, because I knew I had to be accountable to them.

Amigos, My Friends: You Can't Do It Alone

As independent as I am, I know that in order for me to be a truly beautiful and confident person I need other people in my life. In fact, studies show that people who have strong and healthy relationships have a more positive attitude toward life, less stress and are much happier.

KNOW WHO YOUR FRIENDS ARE

In high school I hung out with everyone—the jocks, the smart kids, even the student government crowd. That made it hard to have one or two best friends, but I never felt like I was missing anything and loved that I had such a diverse pool of pals to hang out with.

Once I got to college, that's where I made lifelong best friends I still keep in touch with today. Those friendships helped me learn the difference between the acquaintance-type friends I'd grown up with and the kind of close friends I could confide in and count on for anything.

I also learned that each friend provides a different kind of relationship. There may be one friend who gives great advice about dating. Another friend might be the person you confide in about your most personal and private things. And yet another pal might be the kind of friend who cheers you up and makes you laugh when you're feeling down. Like me when I was in high school, you may discover that you prefer to have lots of friends as opposed to just one or two best friends. Or you might find that you prefer the company of one or two best friends, rather than a large social group. Either is okay—it's just important to have someone that you connect with. And the kinds of relationships you seek may change over time. Today, my sisters, my mom, and my husband are my closest friends because their love is unconditional.

Creating healthy friendships isn't always a walk in the park. For some people, making friends is the hardest part. But you can't just sit around waiting for someone to come over and talk to you. Often, you have to make the first move.

MAKING FRIENDS

I've always been good at making friends and have never had much of a problem meeting new people. I was never really shy, because my family was always having parties and get-togethers where we had to be social—so I was a natural social butterfly. I can start a conversation with pretty much anyone. Not to mention, in my family we learned to have thick skin real fast, so I don't get bent out of shape when people poke fun or get sarcastic with me. I can usually dish it right back, thanks to years of training from my uncles, who teased us mercilessly about everything and anything. Especially the way we looked. One example I'll never forget is the "Crimping Incident." One time I begged my mom to get me a crimping iron so I could style my hair for a big family holiday dinner we were having. I spent an hour on my hair the night of the dinner and thought it totally rocked. My uncles, however, thought otherwise. They laughed at me, saying how ugly my hair was. But I didn't let it bother me. I just brushed off their comments with laughs and said sarcastically, "Oh, yeah. I forgot you were a fashion guru!" (Seriously, you should have seen their hair!) I think because of all their joking around, I was never shy—and could always stick up for myself with a smart comeback.

Another reason I found it easy to make friends was that I

got involved with tons of groups and clubs. To this day I think that's the best way to make friends. Also, the more involved you are in school, the better your college application is—gotta love those extracurricular activities!

Getting Involved

It's important to feel like you belong. And that doesn't mean you have to belong to the most popular crowd or belong to a certain clique. Belonging to a neighborhood, a club, or a team can give you a deep sense of belonging. Plus, doing something that involves your passion can serve two functions: feeding your soul and helping you create strong relationships.

Go Clubbing

When I was a senior, I was part of our high school's Peer Leadership Group. We met once a week and then traveled around to different elementary schools in our area and put on plays about doing good and being an exemplary person. The Peer Leadership Group included all kinds of kids from our school—all of us coming together to send out this positive message. It was really empowering to be a part of the group. Not only did I learn a lot about myself, but I was doing something to give back to the community, and I was making all kinds of new friends.

Get Sporty

I was also really involved in sports. Like I mentioned earlier, I ran indoor and outdoor track and played volleyball.

Having practice every day with the same group of people, you get to know them really well. Plus, you're all working toward the same goal of wanting to win the game, so you really bond. I even found that sometimes teammates who didn't get along before they were on a team together actually learned to get along once they played together. For instance, there were a couple of girls on my team who, for whatever reason, just didn't like each other outside of volleyball. But once they started playing together, and needing each other in order to win—well, they ended up becoming friends. Because we were all working so hard to achieve that win, we forgot about our differences. Through sports you can create relationships that may not have happened otherwise. I became really good friends with girls who were totally different from me—I wouldn't have had the opportunity to even get to know them if I hadn't joined the team.

Work It

Having a job is a great place to meet friends. It's kind of like being part of a team because you all have the same goal—to sell more shirts, get more clients, or write great ad copy—only you're getting paid!

Volunteer

Key #1 focused a lot on how important giving is to cultivating inner beauty. Volunteering can also be a great way to make friends. I made tons of friends when I created Neighborhood Cleanup Days.

What Do You Say?

Introduce Yourself: It may seem awkward, but I often just walk up to someone and introduce myself. I've done this at parties, pageants, and even Hollywood events, and I have made some great friends and connections this way. I know being that bold may not be easy for everyone, and I certainly have times where I'm feeling a bit unsure myself. But I know I have to try, or later I'll probably regret not having made the effort. Often if I've seen the person I'd like to meet at another party or event, I'll approach them and start the conversation that way—"Weren't you at the MTV party last week?" Usually they say yes, they recognize me, too, and we start chatting away. Many of the parties I attend now are full of celebrities. That can be terribly intimidating, but I find if I just act like myself and am very humble I usually get positive reactions. If I'm thrown into a situation with a celebrity whose work I'm familiar with, I'll mention how much I love their new movie or television show or whatever it is they're known for. Soon enough, I'm having a conversation with them.

Take Baby Steps: Everybody has a comfort zone when it comes to being social—even me. I like to imagine my comfort zone as if it's a circle drawn on the ground. That way, if I'm feeling a bit apprehensive, I tell myself that all I have to do is just take one step outside the circle. Then I'll coax myself to take another step, then another, then another. Step by step the comfort zone grows until soon I can talk to just about anyone.

Find Out About Them: People really do love to talk about themselves. Just start asking questions and the conversation will probably have a life of its own. You can start with simple things like "I love your sweater. Where'd you get it?" or "What do you do?" or "Where did you grow up?" Each question can lead to another and then another. This way you really get to know someone—and they'll think you're a great conversationalist.

Make Connections: Notice what you have in common. For instance, does the person live near you? I'm always running into people from my neighborhood at the grocery store, the park, or at events so after seeing them a few times, I introduce myself and then ask them which street or building they live in. Usually that will spark a discussion about stuff to do in the neighborhood, what new restaurants are slated to open soon, or even stories about notorious neighbors.

Smile, *Sonrie*: Always have a smile on your face. Smiling makes you seem happy as well as approachable. A smile makes people feel comfortable about going up and starting a conversation with you. I was always a smiler and found that the more I smiled the more people wanted to be around me and talk to me.

Tell a Joke: Starting off with a joke can be a great way to break the ice. Just remember who your audience is, and don't tell a joke that's inappropriate. And if you need some new jokes, go online. These days you can even have a daily joke texted to your cell!

How to Be a Good Friend

Being a good friend is about being there for one another no matter what—even if you've heard that same darn story over and over (and over!) again. When I was a junior in high school, I had a girlfriend who always went for bad-boy types—even though they were totally wrong for her. She was continually getting her heart broken. It definitely drove me crazy, but I was always there for her—wiping her tears and listening. I learned that I couldn't desert her just because she had a weakness. Sure it was a broken record, and I found I was even repeating the same pep talk: "You're beautiful. You deserve better." I could have easily said, "Why are you doing this to yourself?" But that wasn't what she needed from me. What she needed was a shoulder to cry on and kind, supportive words. I'll admit it took a lot of patience. But I also learned from her what I was capable of giving as a friend.

Being a good friend is part of what builds your character. I found that just being there for my friend, without judgment, even though we'd been through the same scenario dozens of times before, helped me build patience, tolerance, and understanding—not just for her, but for all my friends, my family . . . and even myself.

Friend Fights

Even the best of friends fight sometimes. We have to accept that conflict is just a part of life. Here are some tips I've found useful when handling conflict with friends:

- Learn how to say you're sorry. If you've done something to hurt your friend, fess up and make amends as quickly as possible. Apologize, take responsibility for messing up, and ask what you can do to make things right between the two of you again.
- It's not all about you. Friendships are two-way streets. Make sure you both get equal time in the relationship, and it's not just you doing all the talking and benefiting from the friendship.

- Listen. Perk up your ears and listen to what your *amiga* or *amigo* is telling you. Sometimes we just need to be heard. Learn how to listen without judgment.
- Yay for them! Celebrate your pal's triumphs and successes. It's important to be happy for our friends. This can be difficult when you're both striving for the same goal and only one of you achieves it. But being able to think about *her* instead of *yourself* can actually help you feel better about your situation.
- Don't be a blabbermouth. If your friend confides in you, keep your lips zipped. You wouldn't want her to be spreading your secrets, so be trustworthy and respect her privacy.
- If you are having an argument, ask to talk in private so you can discuss your conflict without an audience. I'm sure you wouldn't like it if she started talking to you in front of all your friends about your disagreement, so wait until you're alone.
- Be honest about how you feel. Don't give a long list of "you said this, you did this." That doesn't solve anything and is only about being right, not about being fair. . . . Let your friend know how what she said made you feel. Chances are, you're probably more hurt and sad than you are mad. Try saying something like "I feel hurt when you talk about me to other people because I thought I was confiding in you." Often your friend may not even realize she did something to hurt you. Whatever it was may not have been intentional, but she still needs to know how it affected you so she won't do it again.
- Cut out the finger pointing. It's easy to say everything is your friend's fault, but try not to blame her. It takes two to tango (I know this from experience!), so you're both involved in the conflict. Even if the argument started because of something your friend did, try to move on from blame and figure out how to fix the situation rather than be righteous about it.
- Make the first move. If you and your friend have an argument,

be the bigger person and call, e-mail, or IM your apology first. You want to get back on track to being close as soon as possible, so extend the olive branch and make the first move toward creating peace.

What to Do When Your Friend Is Facing Something Serious

It's difficult for both you and your friend when she experiences something out of her control. Things like the death or illness of a family member, friend, or pet, a really bad breakup or divorce, the loss of a job, or any number of things can be extremely painful.

Even though there's nothing you can do to prevent these situations from happening, you can be there for your friend. Listening is probably the best way you can help. Sometimes it's hard to know what to say, especially when someone your friend loved has died. It might make you uncomfortable to approach her, but try to put your own feelings of discomfort aside and remember that it's not about you—it's about her. Just tell her, "If you need someone to talk to, I'm here for you." That's all you need to say. Just let her know you care . . . and you're there if she wants to talk.

What Kind of Friend Are You?

1. **Your friend just found out the guy she likes is into someone else. You:**
   a. pump her up with compliments and tell her how awesome she is.

    b. confront the guy and tell him he's really missing out on someone special.

    c. tell your friend it's a great opportunity to meet other fish—lots of other fish.

    d. crack a joke about how he wasn't good enough for her anyway.

2. What's the most important thing about friendship to you?

    a. looking out for each other

    b. giving lots of advice

    c. having lots of people to hang out with

    d. having fun

3. How would you describe your personality?

    a. thoughtful and giving

    b. in charge

    c. bubbly and outgoing

    d. funny

4. What kind of party do you like best?

    a. something small, like a girls' night spa party or movie night

    b. some sort of activity-based party, like bowling or skating

    c. big, huge parties with lots of new people to meet

    d. I am the party

5. To you, school is about:

    a. a place to make good friends.

    b. getting into college.

    c. a nonstop party.

    d. an audience.

6. Your friends say they love you because:

    a. you always know the right thing to say.

b. you always have a plan.

c. you always know where the best parties are.

d. you always make them laugh.

Mostly As: The Nurturer

You're always there when your pals need you. Whether you've got a shoulder to lean on, cookies baking in the oven, or a kind word, your friends know they can turn to you when they need a little lovin'. Just make sure someone's taking care of you, too!

Mostly Bs: The Leader

You're in control. You know what you want out of life, and you know how to get it. Your friends admire your drive and determination. Just remember to soften up now and then, and make sure your girls feel taken care of by you.

Mostly Cs: The Cruise Director

You're the social butterfly of the group—all about having fun. You're the one who plans the Friday night itineraries and looks at every situation as a place to make new friends. Just be careful about over-extending yourself, and be sure to spend lots of downtime being mellow—all those parties can wear a girl out!

Mostly Ds: The Comic Relief

You've constantly got everyone in stitches. You're the practical joker, the class clown, and you've always got something to say that'll ease just about any situation. Your friends love hanging out with you because you make their worries disappear. Just don't forget to be serious sometimes—not everything's a joke!

Friendships Change

It wasn't until college that I had an official "best friend." That was when I met girls I really had a lot in common with. Our bond was unlike anything I had ever experienced before, and I truly felt like we were long-lost sisters. We talked about the future all the time. We planned to be in each other's weddings, play "auntie" to each other's kids, and drink tea together every Sunday once we were grandmothers. It was such an amazing time, and I have great memories of trips we took and funny moments we shared. However, as our lives changed, our relationships changed, too.

Now that I live three thousand miles away from where I grew up and went to college, it's hard to stay as close to my friends as I once could, which is a total bummer. We're no longer roommates with endless amounts of time to hang out and watch *Guiding Light* or *Wedding Story*. Now we have responsibilities (Yikes! the big R word), like home ownership, our careers, and marriages. But even though things have changed, it doesn't mean we still can't be friends. The dynamic is just different now.

Expect your relationships to change as you get older, and don't beat yourself up about friendships not being quite the same as they once were. It took me a long time and countless hours thinking, "Damn, what did I do wrong? Why aren't we talking as much as we used to?" before I realized it wasn't me. I'd done nothing wrong—we were just becoming adults with busy lives and different priorities.

What If Your Best Friend Is a Guy?

In college I had a really good friend who was a guy. It was the first time I ever had a close male friend—my pals were usually always girls. He and I would go to movies together, study together, and grab lunch or coffee together.

It was great because I was able to get a guy's perspective about stuff. I could ask him about guys I liked. "What did he mean when he said he'd call me?" or "Do you think he's into me?" I learned a lot about the way guys think, and I understood them a lot better. It was definitely helpful for dating.

Having a guy friend was easier in some ways than having a girlfriend—girls often have drama—including me! But I noticed that, unlike girls, guys will have an argument, and ten minutes later they're back to being friends and playing video games together. They don't hold on to resentment and bring unresolved issues up later. Once an argument happens, it's over. Issue resolved. They move on, where girls can tend to dwell. That was a great thing to learn because it really helps me to understand my husband better—I know where he's coming from. It also helped with my female relationships, because I tend to let things go now a whole lot quicker than I used to.

So I would definitely recommend having guys as friends—just don't expect them to respond to you the same way your girlfriends do. They probably won't want to spend hours talking about clothes or shopping or gossip.

Also, once you have a boyfriend or your guy friend has a girlfriend, you've got to be willing to adapt the relationship a bit. Your significant other (or his!) might not be comfortable with you hanging out with friends of the opposite sex—even if your friendship is purely platonic. It sucks, but it is important to respect those feelings. One thing you can do to ease the tension is to try to get the two guys to become friends. That way you don't have to give either of them up. And if your tricky situation involves your guy friend's girl, invite her out to dinner or shopping with you so you can get to know each other better and put to rest any fears or insecurities she might have about your relationship with her honey.

Show Your Appreciation

People need to know you appreciate them. It's important to tell friends and family how much they mean to you and that you love them. Think about it—you'd want someone to do the same for you if they thought you were a good friend, right? I love sending little notes or e-cards to let people know how I feel. I can picture them sitting at their desk receiving my card—and that brightens up *my* day. It's so little effort for such a big reward. It's all about feeding the relationship.

Because my mom was both Mom and Dad to us, I always send her a card on both Mother's Day and Father's Day. The Father's Day card always reads, "Thanks for being a great Dad, Mom!!" It's important to me to let her know I recognize how hard she worked and how much she sacrificed for us.

Simple Ways YOU
CAN SHOW SOMEONE YOU APPRECIATE THEM

Send a card, letter, or e-mail just saying something simple like "I'm thinking of you" or "I'm thankful you're my friend."

Pick them flowers.

Call or text them to tell them you love them.

Write a poem just for them.

Take them out to their favorite restaurant for dinner.

Make a mixed CD of their favorite tunes.

Make a photo album or scrapbook of all the fun times that you've had together.

Bake something special to let your friends know how sweet they are. I love to bake a special spice cake when I want to tell my friends "I love you."

SPICE CAKE

CAKE:

1 box of moist spice cake mix

FROSTING:

3 8-ounce packages of regular cream cheese (at room temperature)

6 tablespoons (3/4 stick) unsalted butter (at room temperature)

1½ teaspoons vanilla extract

2½ cups powdered sugar

½ cup crushed ginger snaps

1. Bake the spice cake as directed on the box and let cool off.

2. Beat cream cheese, butter, and vanilla in a large bowl until light and fluffy. Gradually beat in the powdered sugar. Cover and refrigerate until firm enough to spread (about 15 minutes).

3. Spread the frosting on the cake and sprinkle the crushed ginger snaps on top.

4. Enjoy and don't forget to share! You can also serve with a scoop of vanilla ice cream!

Spa Party

Another way to show your friends how much you care is by throwing a spa party. I love doing this! It's also a great way to honor yourself and nourish both your inner and outer beauty. Two weeks before your spa night, send out invitations to all your guests. Keep it simple by sending e-vites. Tell everyone to bring a robe and slippers. You supply all the ingredients, and you and your friends can help one another perform the treatments. Keep plenty of towels on hand.

SPA SERVICES:

(Check out Key #3 for some of these great recipes for spa treatments you and your friends can make at home!)

> *Rosemary steam bath*
> *Rose-petal foot soak with a foot massage*
> *Soothing face mask*
> *Brown sugar scrub*
> *Eye soothers*
> *Olive oil rub*
> *Manicures*
> *Pedicures*

SPA MENU

Keep your menu light and healthy. Spa parties are all about feeling good inside and out, so you don't want to eat anything too heavy. Possible menu items include:

- fresh-cut veggie platter
- mini avocado and sprout sandwiches

- celery sticks with almond butter
- fruit salad
- strawberries and honey—it's one of my faves and perfect for a healthy spa party menu. Slice strawberries in half. Either drizzle with honey or put honey in a bowl and let guests dip.
- the sliced tomato salad from the nutrition section in Key #3
- chilled water with cucumber or strawberry slices. Or you can have two pitchers—one with each so your guests can try both flavored waters. Garnish with a piece of fresh mint.
- refreshing lemon iced tea
- soothing hot chamomile or mint tea

SPA AMBIENCE

This part can be a lot of fun. You can turn your house into a fancy-schmancy zenlike spa. Dim the lights and burn lavender-scented candles to create a relaxing sanctuary for you and your friends. Play your favorite tunes, but make sure nothing is too fast or peppy. You want your guests to feel relaxed, so classical or yoga music is a great choice. A vase of fresh flowers (I like roses) is a nice touch, too, if you want to splurge!

Setting Boundaries

Setting boundaries means creating clear limits with people about how you will and won't be treated. It's up to you to make sure that all of your relationships are based on respect and equality. It took me a long time to figure that out, but it's been essential in terms of creating balanced and healthy relationships in my life.

A few years after my dad left, he showed up again one day and wanted to be back in our lives. For about a month we saw him regularly—he'd take us to dinner or to the gym (I loved going swimming at the gym while my dad lifted weights). It was great. I thought my dad was back in my life forever. Finally, I thought, I had a dad just like everyone else.

But after a month he stopped coming around, he stopped calling, and before I knew it, he was gone again. I didn't understand. A year later he came around again and did the same thing. I got my hopes up. Then he disappeared again. He followed this pattern over and over throughout my childhood: coming around for a little while, then leaving for years.

Finally when I was in college, he said he would take me out to dinner for my birthday. I was so excited to see him. Well, my birthday came and went, and I didn't even get a phone call. That's when I declared "enough." I couldn't let him keep breaking my heart over and over again. I told him I didn't want to see him ever again. It was a hard thing to say, because I wanted to love him, I wanted him around, but I just couldn't take getting hurt anymore. To this day, I don't have a relationship with him, but that's okay. Setting those boundaries made me a much stronger person.

We all need people, but we don't need to have people in our lives who treat us poorly. If you have a friendship that seems unhealthy to you—maybe your friend is bossy, or trying to pressure you to do things you don't want to do. Or maybe she's saying cruel things about you—either behind your back or to your face. Ask yourself these questions:

> *Do I deserve to be treated this way?*
> *Would I treat someone this way?*

Chances are, you'll probably answer no to both questions. When setting boundaries, the first thing you need to do is speak up for yourself.

Speaking Up for Yourself

When the boy in my Spanish class made his nasty remark about Puerto Ricans coming to the U.S. to take advantage of welfare, I couldn't let him get away with it. He was being racist, and insulting me and my family. By explaining my perspective to him, I stood up for myself. He never made a comment like that to me again. Remember, if you don't speak up for yourself, who will? You're your own biggest advocate. If you're being treated unjustly, no one can stick up for you better than you can.

Oprah Winfrey says that "you teach people how to treat you," which I think is really true. It's up to you to make sure people treat you with the love and respect you deserve.

You Don't Have to Be Nice All the Time

Often, as women, we want to please everyone, and we are really conscious of being nice all the time. It's great to be nice, but you shouldn't say yes just for the sake of being nice. It's okay to say no. You're not being mean—you're being real.

You Don't Have to Like Everyone

I always try to be nice to everyone and give each person I meet the benefit of the doubt. But sometimes you will meet people who just aren't very nice. You don't have to like those people. When I was competing for Miss USA, one of the other contestants tried to play head games with me. She came up to me with an odd, falsely concerned look on her face and said, "Susie, do you feel okay?"—implying that I didn't look good. She was trying to knock me off my game. If I hadn't been so prepared, or had low self-esteem, I think I might have run into the bathroom and spent the next half hour freaking out over my hair or my dress or my makeup. Instead, I smiled and said, "I'm GREAT. How are *you* doing?" And then I avoided her for the rest of the competition. Of course I'd say hi if we ran into each other, but otherwise I just steered clear. This girl was obviously not my friend, and there was no reason I needed to go out of my way to make her like me. You just aren't going to like everyone, and vice versa, so it's okay to give yourself permission not to get along with everyone you encounter.

I also learned that people don't always have your best interest at heart—no matter how nice you are. After winning Miss USA 2003, I went on to compete in the Miss Universe 2003 Pageant in Panama City, Panama. If you thought the girls at Miss USA were cutthroat . . . HA! . . . the ones at Miss Universe were even more ruthless. We've all heard stories about girls trying to sabotage one another at pageants, right? Before I witnessed it for myself I thought, "Those stories can't be true." But some were. At Miss Universe, there were a few girls who walked around offering candy to other contestants, though they would never eat any them-selves. I found out they were trying to get the other girls to eat the candy so it would make them bloated, which might make them look bad or not fit into their outfits! Craziness, huh?!

Knowing When You Shouldn't Be Friends with Someone

There are certain people you just shouldn't be friends with. When kids I knew started going down the wrong path—joining gangs and selling drugs—I stopped hanging out with them. I knew that they were going in the complete opposite direction I was, and if I tried to maintain these friendships, they'd throw me off course. And I was all about following the path that would help me achieve my goals and make my dreams come true.

It was sad because one of the girls had been one of my friends since kindergarten. But she started drinking and smoking pot, and that just wasn't me. I didn't approve of her behavior. It was illegal—she could get in trouble, and I didn't want any of that negativity around me, distracting me from reaching my goals.

Of course I was polite when I saw her in our neighbor-hood, and I even gave her a big hug at high school gradua-tion, but I just couldn't be close friends with her.

Sometimes we become friends with people who seem like great friends in the beginning, but really aren't good for you. For a while I had a "friend" who had incredibly high expectations of me. No matter what I did to show her I cared, it was never good enough. She always wanted more: more time, more girls' nights, more phone calls, more . . . I don't even know what! She also wanted full disclosure: it was like she had to know every single thought that passed through my brain and every single minute detail about my entire life. If I didn't check in with her *immediately* to tell her what was going on with me, whether it was a new job, an argument with my husband, or whatever—she'd sarcastically accuse me of being a "private person"—like I was purposely withholding information from her! The crazy part is that she **did** know everything about me, because I'd told her everything so she wouldn't be mad at me!

Plus, she wanted me to spend any free time with her, and would become upset if I had plans with other friends or was too busy with work and couldn't see her. I can't tell you how many times I had to listen to her tell me that I wasn't a thoughtful person. She was like a jealous boyfriend. I was constantly walking on eggshells around her, making sure I said and did all the right things that a friend is "supposed to do" and hoping I wouldn't do anything to piss her off. But it never failed: I did piss her off *all the time.* Nothing was ever good enough for her. So I was a total wreck over the situation—constantly upset or crying because I didn't know what more I could do. I felt like it was my job to make her feel happy, yet both of us were always miserable. It got so bad it was affecting my everyday life—and even my work.

Finally, with the help of my husband, I realized the only way to make the relationship better was to get out of it. So I had to cut my ties with her, which was difficult, but offered me a valuable lesson. Now I steer clear of friends who are too needy or make me feel bad about myself. Nobody needs that in her life.

Breaking Up a Friendship

Sometimes you might need to break up with a friend. It sucks, but if the relationship isn't healthy, you're probably better off apart. If you've talked about your differences and just can't come to a compromise, or the relationship continues spiraling into name-calling and yelling matches, or talking bad about each other behind your backs . . . it's probably time to call it quits.

How do you break up with a friend?

IN PERSON

The best way is face-to-face when you're not angry so you can leave the relationship in a respectful, grown-up way.

ON THE PHONE

Sometimes both friends are too angry, hurt, or emotional to meet in person. So the second-best way is over the phone.

WRITING A LETTER OR AN E-MAIL

And the third-best way is in a letter or e-mail. This works out well because you can get all your feelings and emotions out on paper. And you can proofread it before you send. Just make sure you don't write your letter in anger. You don't want to shoot off an e-mail that will just make the situation worse.

The worst way to break up with anyone is doing it on a Post-it. Remember that episode of *Sex and the City* when Berger broke up with Carrie via Post-it? Not good.

So what do you say? I think it's best to be brief and to the point, and also to be complimentary. Something like:

> I love you, but I think it would be best for both of us if we stopped hanging out. I feel like we're different than we were when we first met, things have changed, and our relationship is making me really sad. I'm going to miss you and our fun times together. Please know that I will always care about you.

Dating

Dating, having a boyfriend, and even marriage definitely require some of the same kind of relationship know-how friendships do. A lot of my advice is the same, but I apply it differently.

I found that dating helped me come out of my shell even more than having friends did. Dating required that I learn to trust people, open up, and become more honest—with others and with myself. Those relationships also reiterated the importance of knowing how to treat people and figuring out how I want to be treated.

GET HIM TO NOTICE YOU

Getting a guy to notice you can take some work. You also have to be prepared for a letdown—in case he likes someone else, already has a girlfriend, or just isn't into you. But the thing is, if you don't try, then you'll never know how he feels about you, and he'll never know how you feel about him. Personally, I always think it's better to wear your heart on your sleeve than keep your feelings all bottled up inside.

Here are some tricks for getting a guy to notice you:

- When you see your crush, shoot him a smile. The next time you see him, say hi. Maybe next time say something longer, like "Hey, what's up!" or "How are ya?" Take it slow until you feel comfortable approaching him.
- Be where he is. Don't be a stalker, but go to the coffee shop where he gets his mochas or attend the same parties he does. The more often he sees you, the more he'll recognize and remember you. I met my high school boyfriend through friends. We all used to go out in groups, so I knew him for about a year before we started going out. So we saw each other ALL the time. One day my friends told me he liked me. I thought he was cute, so we started going out. We had a lot in common since we both came from Latin backgrounds, and he was really into sports, so we had a lot to talk about. My having a boy-friend was tough for my mom to deal with—she didn't want me dating anyone!—so it took her a while to warm up, but after she got to know him better, she was cool with him coming over to watch a movie or letting me go shopping with him.
- Compliment him. If he gets a new haircut, tell him it looks good. You don't have to go overboard, but the point is to let him know you noticed and you think he's special.
- Eye contact. Make sure he sees you looking at him, and give him a smile when his eyes meet yours. Your eyes can say a lot about how you feel. Just don't stare!
- Be his friend. If you already know each other pretty well, let him know you're there for him if he ever wants to talk. This can be risky, though—because if you play the friends card too well, he may think of you as just friends and not

want to ask you out. So try being a "flirty" friend. Eye contact, a sweet smile, and compliments will send the message that you're into him. And hopefully he feels the same way.

WHAT KIND OF GUY IS
Right for Me?

Have you ever thought about what type of guy you're attracted to? Maybe you go for *alto, oscuro y hermoso* (tall, dark, and handsome) ones. Or rugged outdoorsy guys. Or maybe you go for indie rock-star looks. But finding Mr. Right is about a lot more than appearance—it's about discovering what qualities and characteristics you're attracted to.

Check off the following in order of importance, from 1 to 3—1 being the most important and 3 being the least:

Sense of humor
Kind
Helps others
Intelligence
Ambitious
Adventurous
Courteous
Good-looking
Generous

Dresses with flair
Athletic
Loves animals
Sensitive
Reserved
Outgoing
Popular
Vegetarian
Conservative
Environmentalist
Into money
Open-minded
Fun

Now see which traits have the most 1s in front of them. These are the characteristics you should look for in a boy. Now look at the qualities you put a 3 next to. This is what you *don't* want in a date.

Before I was married I always kept a list of what qualities were most important to me in a mate. I used them to guide me. If the person I was seeing didn't have at least three of the traits I thought were important—or had three or more traits I was not attracted to—I had to say buh-bye. I wasn't trying to be mean. I was just trying to save us both grief and heartache later on. Why would I go out with someone who doesn't live up to my standards? Then I'm always going to be wishing he were someone else and trying to get him to change, which is totally unfair.

OKAY, I'VE GOT HIS ATTENTION—NOW WHAT?

This is the fun part—getting to know each other! Once he knows you've got eyes for him, there are some things to keep in mind when moving on to the next step, which is (hopefully) going out with him.

Invite him to group gatherings or parties. If you and your pals are going to the movies, ask him to come along and bring his best friend. This is a great way to get to know him better without too much pressure. Also, if you're hosting a party, be sure to invite him.

If he's shy, ask him out. It's not that big of a deal anymore if a girl asks a guy out. Sometimes guys just need a little encouragement. Don't ask a friend to ask him out for you—that always turns out bad. Plus, it makes you look like you don't have any courage!

Always be yourself. Don't wear a lot of makeup if you don't normally, or dress up in fancy clothes if you're normally a jeans and T-shirt kind of girl. Sure, if you're going to the prom—that's different. But don't change who you are for anyone. That also applies to your personality—you don't have to be a chatty social butterfly if you're normally more mellow and casual.

Stay true to yourself. Stand up for what you believe in, even if he doesn't agree. It's okay to listen to other points of view, but don't change your opinion just for him. He's going to respect you for having your own voice.

Speak up. Don't be afraid to tell him how you feel or to disagree with him. If you didn't like the movie and he did, that's okay. You don't have to feel the same way about everything all the time. Who does?

Look your best. Wear your favorite outfit, and make sure

you're clean, neat, and not wrinkled. Like I said, don't all of a sudden become a supermodel if you're usually a jock—but putting a little effort into how you look will show him that you care.

Make conversation. Stuck about what to say? The easiest way to start a conversation is to talk about *him*. Ask who his favorite bands are, what his favorite movie is, what his career plans are. Don't talk to him about stuff you'd normally talk to your girlfriends about, like who wore what, or how the Gap is having a sale on leggings. He'll most likely tune you out. This doesn't mean you can't talk about yourself, but stick to subjects that you have in common or that you know he's interested in. Try not to ask questions that could be answered with a simple yes or no—ask questions that inspire him to open up.

Laugh. Be sure to laugh at his jokes, and go ahead and tell some of your own if you're also a jokester. (If you're normally a more serious person, don't put pressure on yourself to be a comedian. Just be relaxed and enjoy his humor if he's funny.)

Remember to breathe. If you happen to get nervous take a couple of deep breaths to calm yourself. And remember, he's probably just as nervous as you are. Feel free to crack a joke about it—it'll make you seem comfortable with yourself, even if you're not.

GREAT DATES

You don't have to go anywhere superexpensive to have a fun date. Here are some of my favorite date suggestions:

- a picnic in the park
- going to the movies
- renting a movie and making popcorn

- going for a walk
- studying together
- hanging out at the mall
- sharing an ice-cream sundae (cute and so retro!)
- going out for burgers or pizza (I love bacon cheeseburgers and spicy pizzas with sausage, pepperoni, onion, and peppers—yum!)
- apple picking (then you can go home and bake a pie if you want and continue the date!)
- going to a carnival
- ice-skating if it's winter time
- hanging out at the beach (P.S. Learn how to throw a football. Guys like to do that at the beach, and it's fun.)
- And here's one that he'll definitely be impressed by: invite him over to watch a sports game! (I love to watch NFL games. The New England Patriots are my home team, so every Sunday in the fall and winter, you can find me sitting on a couch watching the game. My man and I usually invite some friends over and make some goodies.)

Dating DON'TS

- Don't dress like a hoochie mama. If you want a guy to like you for who you are and respect you, be careful how you go about attracting him. Some girls think that by wearing skimpy clothes and acting overly flirtatious, it'll get guys to notice. They may be right, in the sense that guys will take notice, but they'll attract the wrong kind of guy. If you dress like a hoochie, you'll get treated like one. Remember the laws of attraction!

- Don't talk about yourself too much.
- Don't get too serious. Talking about serious issues like politics and world events when you don't know each other well can make a situation tense.
- Don't talk about the future. Don't think that because you're on this date now that you two will be getting married next year and having a family. That's way too much to decide now! Just concentrate on how much fun you're having in the present, and let the future happen as it comes.
- Don't have wandering eyes. Keep your attention focused on him—even if there are other cute guys at the party, you're there with him. It's rude and disrespectful to check out other people.
- Don't talk about other boys you liked or dated. TMI—he doesn't need a rundown of your playbook. It makes it seem like you're living in the past rather than enjoying your time with him now.
- Don't get obsessive. Let him know you like him and then back away. Calling or texting him a thousand times a day will make you seem like a stalker and will make him want to bolt.
- Don't do anything you don't want to do. When you say no, mean it. And make sure he understands. Don't let him talk you into something that's against your wishes. If he pushes, the date is over. Ask him to take you home immediately or walk away to somewhere safe and call a friend to pick you up.
- Don't dump on him. If you've had a bad day, try to shake it off and greet him with a big smile anyway. Don't show up for your date complaining.
- Don't settle for someone who doesn't make you happy. There's

no reason to go out with a guy who's "good enough"—you want to go out with someone who's great!

- Don't date bad boys! They'll just break your heart. I have always steered clear of bad-boy types. I just don't want to date anyone who's into being rowdy and getting in trouble and treating me like crap. Before I was married, when I was interested in a guy, I would ask around to find out who he hung out with. If it was a crowd that was into drugs or just up to no good I immediately crossed him off the list. I just didn't want that trouble in my life.

WHAT IF HE DOESN'T LIKE YOU?

There was a guy in my sophomore English class who I had a major crush on—in fact, I was into this guy from seventh grade on. We had lots of classes together, and since his last name started with a B, he always sat somewhere near me. Once we got accused of cheating on a test—we didn't, but we'd answered the same question almost exactly the same way, so the teacher suspected us. She made us stay after school and take the test over again. I actually thought this was great because I got to spend time talking to him. That was when I found out he already had a girlfriend—and she was absolutely nothing like me. So I realized I wasn't his type. *Que lastima!* It was a bummer, but good to know so I could move on.

My best advice for how to deal when a guy you like isn't into you is to be proud of yourself for making the effort, and then quickly get over it, and set your sights on someone else. It's not like you can give your wannabe guy a love potion (although that sounds cool, huh!?!) to make him fall for you. Mami used to say to me, "If he doesn't like you, someone else will." And she was right. Look around you—the world is filled with great guys! Maybe there's even someone right under your nose.

Also, realize that sometimes maybe you guys are better off as just friends.

Dating Dilemmas

FIGHTING

Just like in other relationships, disagreements between you and yours truly are inevitable. Sometimes we just don't get along—even if we really love someone. But I've got some tips to help you deal when you find yourselves on opposite sides of an argument:

- Be calm. Try not to yell at each other. If you're angry, count to ten and come back when you're composed.
- Be clear and timely. Tell him what he did *this time* that made you angry; don't bring up every other thing he did that hurt you in the past. It's too much to deal with at once.
- If he's mad at you, listen to his concerns with respect, patience, and love. Remember he mostly wants you to hear him and assure him that you still care about him. The best thing you can do when you've done something wrong is to listen, tell him you're sorry, and ask what you can do to make him feel better.
- If you're fighting on the phone, never hang up on him. Don't slam the phone down in anger while he's midsen-

tence. It's completely rude and disrespectful, and will just make him even more angry.

- Don't threaten to break up with him if you don't mean it. This is a cruel and hurtful tactic that serves no purpose except to make both of you more upset. If you really do want to break up with him, you better mean it.
- Be respectful, even when you're arguing. Don't say nasty things to each other, like calling each other names or bringing up each other's insecurities—then you're just bringing more things to fight about into the argument.
- Discuss problems in person, not through e-mail. As great as e-mail can be for expressing feelings, having an e-mail fight isn't a good idea because we often misread language when it's written instead of spoken.
- Be sure to listen to his side. Both of you need to be heard.
- Say it. Don't keep your feelings bottled up and expect that he's going to guess how you feel or what you're thinking. You have to tell him.

It also helps to have a few relationship "rules." This ensures that you both know what's expected of the other and actually makes dealing with conflict less likely to get out of control. Here's what my husband and I have promised each other:

- Never go to bed mad and always say, "I love you," before going to sleep.
- Always give each other a kiss before we leave the house—or as often as possible (fun!).
- Keep serious discussions private and do not include friends or family in our issues.

The last one is essential to us and should be to you, too. When you complain about your guy to your girlfriends or to your mom, they're going to be getting a one-sided description of your partner. Eventually, if you tell them all the negative stuff, they may decide they don't like your significant other. And that doesn't help your relationship. In some cases, it might make it worse. Think about it: even once the problem has been solved, in the future, your friend or family member may only remember the bad stuff you told them about your mate. You want their advice to be balanced, not biased against your significant other.

If you and your partner can't solve an issue, it may be time to meet with a professional, like a couples counselor or therapist. A professional will hear both sides of the story in an open, healthy environment and give you unbiased advice.

BREAKING UP

Sometimes a relationship just doesn't work out. Either you've changed, or he's changed, or you've both changed, or the relationship has just run its course, and it's time to move on.

No one enjoys a breakup. Whether you're the one doing the breaking up, or you're the one who gets broken up with—both experiences are difficult and emotional.

When I was a freshman in college, I broke up with my high school boyfriend. We'd gone out for three years, and I was really trying to concentrate on school, volleyball, and modeling, so I just didn't feel that having a boyfriend was the right thing for me at that time in my life. You have to invest a good amount of time into a relationship, and free time was lacking during that period of my life. Another thing that made us grow apart is that I always wanted big things for my future and was ambitious, and he wasn't even planning to attend college. So our paths were kinda going in different directions. But telling him it was over was torture for me, especially because we were such great friends.

Here's how I did it—this may help you if you're ever in this situation.

First, I called and told him we needed to meet and have a "talk." I wanted to actually tell him in person, because, in my opinion, when you break up with someone you were once in love with, you owe him the respect of actually talking to each other face-to-face. I would never recommend breaking up with a boyfriend through e-mail or over the phone.

Then I thought about all the reasons why we were breaking up. I wanted to be prepared in case he had any questions for me. I didn't want to have too many reasons, but I wanted to have a few so that he would understand how serious I was.

We met on campus, and I told him I wanted to break up. I let him know that it was a really difficult decision and that I still cared for him a great deal, but I needed a change.

Both of us cried for a while, but he also knew it was the right thing to do. We promised to remain friends, then hugged and went our separate ways.

For a while I avoided places I knew he'd be. We both needed time to adjust and get used to our new "friends" status. Seeing each other so soon after the split would just be too hard.

I also stopped calling him. I knew we needed a clean break, and if we kept talking on the phone, we'd just be dragging out our breakup.

I actually felt pretty good about how our breakup went. Friends of mine had experienced much worse. Some had guys yell at them. Others heard guys promise to change and begged them to not break up. In those situations you have to stick to your guns and be insistent about what you want. Don't stay with someone because you feel sorry for him. You're just going to end up breaking up with him at a later date.

GETTING OVER A BREAKUP

Sometimes, we're the ones who get dumped. And that sucks just as much as being the dumper.

When I was in college, my then-boyfriend had many things happening in his life that were scary and overwhelming. He decided that being in a committed relationship wasn't what was best for him and broke up with me after six months of dating. I didn't see it coming, so I was shocked. I cried a lot and called Mami often. Every chance I got, I would drive home or spend some much-needed time with my girlfriends, immersing myself in other activities. One of my roommates, whose actual home was just forty-five minutes away, had girls' nights with our favorite yummy sandwiches, chicken-finger subs, and homemade s'mores, which I would make in the microwave anytime I needed them (talk about a great friend to host a girls' night whenever any of our friends wanted one!). We would go to the movies or shopping (retail therapy can cure almost any ailment!)—anything to get my mind off the hurt I felt.

I tried to avoid my ex at all costs, but that was tricky because we both lived in the same dorm on campus and both worked out at the college gym, so I still saw him all the time. Talk about painful! It was awful.

Time went by, and I still missed and cared for him. I evaluated our relationship before the breakup and asked myself, "Did the good times outweigh the bad?" The answer was "yes" so I decided to ask him how *he* felt about our relationship and see if he wanted to give it another shot. I risked being hurt yet again if the answer was "no" but I thought, "No guts, no glory!"—if I didn't ask I would never find out if he felt the same way I did. I had to work up the courage to talk to him and prepare myself to let go of the relationship forever if he didn't share the same feelings. One day we went for a walk and after talking for a while, he ended up apologizing for breaking up with me. He said that he realized how much he loved me, which were feelings that he never felt before, and that scared him. We decided to get back together and give the relationship another try.

With work our relationship got better and better after that. We went out for years—he was with me through my reign as Miss USA—and eventually I married him! He actually proposed on national television while I was on the show *On-Air with Ryan Seacrest* promoting the Miss USA 2004 pageant with all fifty-one of the contestants. There was a lot of running mascara that afternoon! He's my best friend, and I love him more than words can describe. Suffice to say, I'm glad we worked it out and gave the relationship a second chance!

Always trust your gut feeling. If you want to give someone a second chance after they've messed up, ask yourself these questions:

> *Did the good times outweigh the bad?*
> *Can you trust him again after what he did? (Hopefully it wasn't anything major.)*

If you choose not to give him a second chance because perhaps the bad times outnumbered the good—remember that eventually, like the saying goes, time heals your wounds. After some time passes, it won't hurt quite as much when you see him, even if his boyish good looks still make your heart thump. Until, finally, you won't feel a thing for him at all.

Here's what got me through my toughest breakup:

- Lots of Kleenex. It's okay to cry. Let yourself feel the pain and cry as much and as often as you need to. It's best to get it all out.

- Gathering the girls. Make sure you have your support system of friends and family there with shoulders ready. This is when your network of relationships really counts. And you should count on your pals to be there for you.
- Getting mad. You are probably going to be angry and feel like you want to scream or yell. Why did this happen to me? Why did he do it? It's okay to be angry—it's normal, but try not to dwell on the situation. Don't go after him in a jealous rage and slash his tires, or try to hack into his e-mail and find out who he's dating. Sure, the temptation might be there. But resist. Be strong. Instead, write down everything that pissed you off about the relationship, your ex and the breakup, and then tear up the letter and throw it away. It should help you let go of some of the rage. Take a kickboxing class at the gym. I used to pretend that I was smacking my ex-boyfriend every time I hit a volleyball in practice! Yup! It was a fantastic way of letting out my anger without hurting anyone.
- Staying busy. Get involved in other things. Hang out with your friends a lot. Go to the gym. Hike. Read a book. Take up a new hobby. Do things that will get you out of your own head. Hanging out in your room all the time moping, listening to sad songs, and analyzing what went wrong will just make getting over him more difficult.
- Not rushing. Getting over someone takes time. Let yourself grieve for as long as it takes. You don't have to rush right into another relationship.
- R-E-S-P-E-C-T. Respect for yourself. Remember who you are—you're a great person. He didn't value you enough. But you love yourself, and someday you'll find someone who cares about you as much as your friends, family, and you do.
- Letting go . . . going, going, gone. One day you wake up, and the pain is gone. Just like that. And you realize you

really didn't want to be with someone who didn't love and treat you the way you deserved to be treated.

- Thinking of it as a new beginning. This is a tough one, but if you can—look at your breakup as a new beginning. You now have the opportunity to try new things, meet new people, and take new chances.
- Inner strength. Breakups can also make us stronger. You survived. You got through it. You can do anything. Tell yourself, "I don't need a boyfriend." After my breakup I found I was completely okay on my own. Having a boyfriend didn't define who I was. Sadly, some of my friends— especially back when we were in high school and college—don't feel good about themselves unless they have a guy interested in them. Well, that's just plain wrong. Having a boyfriend can be a lot of fun—don't get me wrong—but having a guy doesn't make you smarter or more beautiful or a better person. You are all those things on your own.
- Personal playlist. I used to keep a collection of tunes on hand just for soothing heartbreaks or any bad times. If I was feeling kind of vengeful, I'd turn up Alanis Morissette's "You Oughta Know" or Beyoncé's "Me, Myself and I." If I was more in the mood to have a good cry, I'd put on Maroon 5's "Sweetest Goodbye" or Gwen Stefani's "Cool."

Inner Beauty Is All About You and Me

You can see why embracing and nurturing your relationships are so important to developing who you are and unlocking your inner beauty. Relationships open us up and reflect back to us who we are and who we can be.

Remember...

IT TAKES TEAMWORK: In order for your family "team" to be successful, you've got to be able to communicate, be patient and willing to compromise, have respect for one another, trust one another, and set aside plenty of family time for fun activities and bonding.

FIND A MENTOR: Seek an authority figure who can help, inspire, and guide you.

YOU CAN'T DO IT ALONE: It's important to have friends to get us through the good times and the bad times.

GET INVOLVED: Make friends by getting involved in clubs, sports, a job, or by volunteering.

BE A GOOD FRIEND: Friends are supportive, loving, honest, and there for one another.

SHOW YOUR APPRECIATION: Let your loved ones know you care by sending them notes, cards, or other tokens of your affection.

SET BOUNDARIES: Be honest with yourself and others about what you will and won't accept in your relationships.

SPEAK UP: Don't keep feelings bottled up inside.

YOU DON'T HAVE TO BE FRIENDS WITH EVERYONE: You can be nice to everyone, but that doesn't mean you have to be best buds with everyone. Some people may not be your type or may be too negative for you.

By this point in the book, you understand how important it is to develop and nurture your relationships with yourself and those who you love and support. Following the first two keys will provide you with both a sense of self-stability and a positive support system of people who honor and nurture you, as well.

You can now use the tools indicated in Key #2 to create new relationships or hone existing ones or end a bad one. To this day, I continue to follow these guidelines. For example, I still get nervous sometimes when I go to Hollywood parties, where I have to schmooze and network with other guests in order to advance my career. There are times when I have to step outside my comfort zone and introduce myself to people I don't know. That can be pretty scary! By using the exercise where I imagine a circle on the floor that expands as my comfort level increases I can usually get through those anxious situations.

Call on Key #2 when you're making new friends and trying to determine if they're right for you. If they're not, or your personalities just don't gel, it's okay to move on. Always speak up for yourself, remembering that you don't have to be nice to everyone, and set boundaries so that your relationships have very clear limits and expectations. If you have to break up a friendship, keep my tips in mind and try to do it in a gentle yet firm way.

You can turn to Key #2 when it comes to dealing with your sweetie, as well. Communication and understanding go a long way toward creating a positive and healthy experience with your significant other. As your relationships get more serious, it's essential to have the right communication skills. Even though I'm married now, I have to work at nurturing our marriage all the time, making sure we spend plenty of quality time together, have room for romance, and connect with each other on a day-to-day basis, as well as on a deeper level. Even if you and your honey get along great, you still need to be willing to put lots of time and effort into the relationship.

Having learned both of the first two keys, you are now ready to move on to Key #3, which is one of my favorite parts of this plan! It's all about unlocking your personal power and recognizing that you're the one in control of looking and feeling your best.

when *I was fourteen I decided I wanted to be a* model for real. No more cat-walking our apartment hallway—I wanted to try the real deal. But there was a lot I needed to learn. First of all, how would I transform my usual tomboy self into a glamour girl? How would I figure out what to wear (and what *not* to wear)? And, how in the heck do those eyelash-curler thing-a-ma-jiggers work? Seriously, I was pretty clueless. I knew how I *wanted* to look, but I had no idea how to get there.

My family offered a lot of moral support, but they couldn't really give me any advice. Neither Mami nor Mama Lola knew a thing about clothes, hair, or makeup. Their focus was on family and providing a good life for us. If I wanted to be a model, it was my job to learn how. So I studied. A lot.

I flipped through magazines to see what was "in" and to discover the latest trends. I also watched a lot of runway shows and photo shoots on E! (back then E! was all about fashion) to learn how to pose, how to walk, and how to dress.

I started experimenting with my makeup and hair, and practiced by copying styles I saw in *Seventeen* and *Vogue*. I began to take more of an interest in my appearance, and spent a little more time getting ready.

Through my investigations, I discovered that a classic, sophisticated, yet sporty style works best for me. I might even say that I tend toward dressing more on the preppy or conservative side. I picked Julia Roberts as my fashion role model. Her sophisticated yet simple style appealed to me. What I admired about her was that no matter what she wore—whether it was a beautiful evening gown or something casual—it was always *Julia Roberts* wearing the clothes rather than the *clothes* wearing Julia Roberts. I also discovered what styles don't work on me. For instance, clothes that are too "edgy" just come off looking totally wrong and don't show off my best assets. I think people who wear really loud clothes or trends that are too Goth or punk are often overshadowed by their outfits. Instead of wearing the *right* clothes to show off their personalities, they seem to wear the *wrong* clothes, which make them seem like they're either hiding themselves or trying too hard. I wanted to find a style that made me look good and showed off my personality.

Obviously, my research and practice paid off, because I did become a model at age fourteen and then, of course, went on to become Miss Massachusetts Teen USA and then Miss USA.

I have to say, learning how to look good is totally empowering. I saw myself blossom both outside *and* inside. My transformation was fun and exciting, and it definitely boosted my self-confidence, which is what enhances true beauty. Plus, the biggest bonus for me was discovering that my health and body image were totally up to me—I was the one who had the power to revamp myself!

In this section I show you how taking control of your

health and body image is all up to you. I share the health and beauty secrets I acquired along the way and invite you to try them and see which ones work for you.

You'll see how, with just a bit of research, practice, and a little extra getting-ready time, you, too, can attain ultimate beauty. I'm not talking about typical beauty that you see on the airbrushed celebs in magazines. I want to inspire you to find your own unique beauty. I believe that every woman can be beautiful. She just needs to know how to enhance her assets to make herself gorgeous.

You'll learn how I went from having a mullet to Miss USA. I share my basic beauty regimen, which includes steps as easy as getting plenty of sleep and drinking lots of water. And I explain the importance of good nutrition for maintaining optimal weight and well-being. You'll learn why a diet plan full of organic fruits and veggies is a must for both looking good and feeling great. I even share some of my favorite healthy recipes—ones that are yummy and good for you, too! Then I get you moving by introducing you to a few workout moves. You'll learn a little yoga, Pilates, and even salsa.

Behind every gorgeous girl is a beauty playbook, one that includes an arsenal of makeup, skin-care treatments, and hair products. I reveal what's in my own makeup bag and show you how to apply makeup for both day and night. You'll also figure out which hairstyle works best on your face shape, and I teach you how to style your locks into glamorous dos worthy of the red carpet. Plus, I clue you in on some beauty pageant secrets. Ever heard of Butt Glue? You will now!

Clothes can reveal a lot about who you are. In this section, you'll also find out how I learned what to wear, as well as what not to wear. You'll be encouraged to develop a signature style and learn how to determine what styles, cuts and colors look best on your body type. I also disclose my slimming secrets—tricks I use for trimming those extra five pounds the camera adds. And I help you pick out the perfect outfit for every occasion, whether you're going to a party, a job interview, or just hanging with the girls.

Finally, I give you tips for learning how to love your look, no matter what shape, style or size you are. True beauty requires being confident about the style choices you make. My advice will inspire you to be proud of who you are and how you look, and encourage you to strut your stuff like a runway diva!

Key #3

TAKE CONTROL OF YOUR *Health* AND *Body Image*

PHOTO BY CARMEN CINTRÓN

Behold! The mullet...my NOT so cool stage.
But it's funny to look at, huh?!

Taking control of your health and body image is the next step toward unlocking your true beauty. Being in charge of how you feel and how you look will help build your inner strength and confidence. You're kind of like a beautiful cake: you have all the right ingredients—you just need a little frosting to add the final touch!

Now that you understand how developing your spirituality and embracing relationships contribute to your inner beauty, you're ready to focus on your outer beauty. But remember, it's still about what's inside that's most beautiful. All the secrets and tips I'm going to tell you don't really work unless you've mastered the first two keys, but learning how to look your personal best will help both your inner and outer beauty. When we look good, we feel good, and when we feel good, we look good.

You do not have to be a stick-thin supermodel or a supercurvy diva to look good. Looking good is about being healthy and looking your personal best. That's what I'm going to teach you how to do, because that's what I had to learn.

You've probably seen casting calls, or go-sees, on *America's Next Top Model.* That's how I had to start—going on auditions with casting directors in the hope that they'd like my look and hire me to be in their commercials or catalogues. I had only one chance to make a first impression, and I learned real quick dressing down in sweatpants wasn't going to help me make the right first impression!

Those modeling auditions taught me some valuable first-impression tips that I still follow today when going on auditions or interviews or to meetings.

Keep it classic. When I went on auditions, I dressed fashionably, but refrained from wearing anything too trendy. Sometimes I would add one accessory that was in that season, like a scarf or a pair of earrings, to show I was up-to-date with current styles, but not a slave to fashion. Once I started going on auditions regularly, my agent would often let me know ahead of time what the casting directors were looking for so I could dress appropriately. Like if it was for a sporting goods store, I'd wear a more athletic outfit. If the audition was for a more conservative department store, I'd dress more conventionally.

Wear muted colors that complement you. Skip the fuchsia pumps or lime green jacket. You want people to remember *you*, not the color of your clothes.

Fling the bling. Don't wear big or sparkly jewelry. Just like bright colors, they distract from you.

When I competed in the pageants, I had to learn yet another way to dress and style myself. With modeling, anything goes, from mainstream to high fashion to avant-garde, but in pageants, girls are expected to be more bubbly and cutesy—especially for the teen competitions. The image they wanted was very innocent and wholesome.

To learn all things pageant, I had to train—just like when I got ready for a track meet or volleyball game. So I hired a coach—yep, they actually have coaches for pageants. They even have shops that specialize in pageant wear, like swim-suits, gowns, shoes, and jewelry. I met my coaches—the mother and daughter team of Maria and Michelle—at the Crowning Touch in New Bedford, about two hours from our house. They taught me everything—from how to walk in swimsuit and evening gown to picking out the best colors for my skin tone.

Here's a pageant tip I found really interesting: Maria always made sure the length of my gown just grazed the floor. The reason is because when delegates are onstage, we're higher than the judges. If the dress was two inches shorter, from the judges' angle, it would appear much shorter. The wrong length dress can make you look sloppy. Who knew!?

So I went from being a sporty athlete to a sophisticated beauty queen. It proved to me that anyone can become glam-orous as long as she has the right skills and is willing to make an effort, and maybe even some sacrifices along the way.

The beauty wisdom I gained through my modeling and pageant experiences has become even more valuable as my ca-reer progresses. Each new role I've landed—from being an MTV VJ to spokesperson for Neutrogena—has been successful, I believe, because of what I've learned and can now practice.

Health and Beauty

Health and beauty go together like Mami's rice and beans! That's because being healthy *is* beautiful. To possess true beauty, you can't have one without the other. Even though

I definitely know a lot of beauty secrets, it's important to start off with the basics. The good-sense rules I follow have nothing to do with makeup or hair spray. They're essential guidelines that form the foundation of any health-and-beauty regimen. In addition to having goal-oriented mantras, I've also created a health-and-beauty mantra, which I tell myself when I'm having one of those not-feelin'-so-gorgeous days: I have the power to create who I am—both inside and out.

PLENTY OF SLEEP

Experts call it "beauty sleep." Well, it really is. Getting enough rest contributes to both your inner and outer beauty. I try to get nine hours a night. Of course, that doesn't always happen if I have to work late or I'm traveling, but most nights I'm in bed by midnight, and I wake up between eight thirty and nine a.m. I find if I don't get enough sleep, my eyes are puffy and I'm sluggish all day. If you have a hard time getting to sleep at a reasonable time, try drinking a cup of noncaffeinated tea, like chamomile, before bed. I like it with a little drop of honey. It's soothing and so yummy! My favorite tea is the Art of Tea, which I order online. You can find it at artoftea.com.

LOTS OF WATER

Water is great for your skin and also for maintaining your weight. It used to be recommended that everyone should have eight glasses of water a day, but those rules have changed and you might not need that much. If you're eating a healthy diet full of lots of fruits and vegetables, you'll get some of your water intake from your food. As long as you drink a few glasses of water per day, you're probably at a good level of hydration, which boosts your health and helps your skin look good.

REMOVE YOUR MAKEUP BEFORE BED

This is a biggie! Remove all makeup every night—even if you get home late or are really tired. Leaving makeup on overnight can lead to pimples and premature wrinkles. Plus, it'll stain your pillowcase. You can use soap and water to remove most makeup, but some mascaras—especially waterproof ones—usually won't come off unless you use eye-makeup remover. If you don't have any eye-makeup remover, drop a small dab of moisturizing face lotion on a cotton ball and gently wipe your lashes. Don't rub too hard—you don't want to get the solution in your eyes or damage the sensitive skin around the eye area. I wash my face in the morning and at night regardless of whether I'm wearing makeup, just to wash away the day's buildup of pollution, oil, and dirt.

SMILE☺

A pageant girl's trademark is her smile. Sometimes I got worried my mouth would stay stuck that way! So I know a lot about the importance of having a healthy smile. Not only is a bright smile important in terms of how you look, but oral hygiene is vital to good health. People who don't take care of their teeth are more prone to infection and disease. (Yuck!)

Smiles are also essential when making a first impression. People notice a bright white smile. Make sure you brush twice a day—my dentist told me to count to sixty before I stop brushing—and floss before bed. I also like to rinse with a plaque-fighting mouthwash. To keep my teeth nice and white, I sometimes have them professionally bleached, but I use those whitening strips you can buy at the drug store. I also cut back on drinks that stain teeth, like coffee, red wine, and teas.

Smile

FOR THE CAMERA

Here's a smile secret I learned while doing pageants. A dab of Vaseline on your teeth helps keep you grinning all night long. Competitions would often last two or three hours—and that meant lots of smiling, which can get pretty exhausting, not to mention your mouth can get really dry. Vaseline helps your pucker stay moist and keeps lipstick off your teeth. This is a great trick if you're going to be somewhere where a lot of pictures are going to be taken—like at the prom or your aunt's wedding.

Stretch

Stretching wakes up your muscles and can help your body relax. I like to stretch every morning when I wake up and every night before I get my zzz's. And I always stretch before and after a workout to make sure I don't strain any muscles. Here are a couple of my favorite stretches:

Good Morning

SUNSHINE STRETCH

Stand up tall with your arms at your sides.

Raise your arms to touch above your head.

Bend at the waist and let your hands touch the floor. If they don't reach, let them dangle.

Hold for three counts.

Rise back to standing, raising your arms at the same time until they touch above your head.

Then bring your arms back to your sides.

Repeat five to ten times.

Good Night

MOON STRETCH

Sit on the floor with your legs in a V.

Bend over your right leg, reaching for your ankle or foot.

Try to touch your forehead to your knee.

Hold for five counts.

Repeat on the left side.

Posture

As a host and actress, I have to pay really close attention to my posture. You'd be surprised at how much posture can affect someone's appearance. Sitting and standing straight can make you look taller, more slender, radiant, and confident. Someone who slouches all the time can look older, heavier, unattractive, and insecure. Plus, bad posture can wreak havoc on your bones and muscles. When you're standing, think of growing taller, like a tree. Push your shoulders back and lift your chin just a bit. It may feel weird at first—like you're sticking your chest out too far, but you're not. Try straightening your posture and slouching in front of a mirror so you can see the difference.

Healthy Routine

For me, having a routine helps me stay balanced. Washing my face, brushing my teeth, and stretching before bed keeps me focused and on track. It's also comforting and always ensures a good night's sleep. Showering, washing my hair, and putting on makeup in the morning wakes me up and gives me a jolt of energy for the day. When I travel or work late, and my routine gets out of whack, so do I. I really notice a difference in the way I feel, which then affects the way I look.

Nutrition

What you eat impacts everything about you—your mood, energy level, brain power, how you feel, and of course how you look. Like everything else in life, when it comes to nutrition, it's important to have balance.

I thank my lucky stars that I was blessed with a tall and slim body type. But I do need to exercise and eat well to stay in shape. It's important for me to be toned and fit—and that takes work and dedication. So what I eat is critical to my health-and-beauty regimen—which of course benefits my inner beauty.

When I first started modeling and competing in pageants I met with a nutritionist/trainer who suggested things for me to eat. Back then I'd have three hard-boiled eggs, minus two yolks, and a piece of toast with peanut butter for breakfast. I also started introducing a lot more fruit and veggies to my diet. I found that the better I ate, the better I felt, and the better I looked. Everything seemed to be connected. And nothing proves that more to me than the way I eat now.

I follow an eating plan that incorporates what I've learned from my brilliant, lifesaving nutritionist, Natalia Rose, who wrote *The Raw Food Detox Diet.* It's not a "diet" like the South Beach Diet or low-carb diet or the grapefruit diet, which seem to be temporary fixes. There's no "dieting." It's about making a lifestyle change and eating healthier forever.

You're probably thinking, "Raw food? Does Susie eat only raw vegetables?" No. I love a big, juicy steak every now and then, and I eat fish and chicken, too. I do eat cooked food, and I even indulge in chocolate. Cutting out foods I love is not what this eating plan is about. The plan helps me focus on what my body needs to function properly. I pay close attention to the quality of the food I buy and properly combine what I eat so that my body can easily digest it. Natalia taught me that properly combining meals helps the body digest food more easily, allowing it to function more efficiently, like a well-oiled machine! I highly recommend that you check out her Web site www.therawfooddetoxdiet.com and pick up her book, because I'm sure you'll be just as enlightened.

BREAKFAST BOOST

I never skip breakfast. *Ever.* Having breakfast helps me stay alert, keeps me focused, and gives me energy. You're probably going to wrinkle your nose when I tell you what I eat—or actually, drink—every morning, but it's delicious, I swear! It's from *The Raw Food Detox Diet* and requires a juicer, which is my favorite kitchen appliance.

GREEN LEMONADE

1 serving

1 head of romaine lettuce or celery

5 to 6 stalks of kale (any type)

1 to 2 apples (as needed for sweetness—Natalia recommends organic Fuji)

1 whole organic lemon (you don't have to peel it)

1 to 2 inches of fresh ginger (optional)

Process everything in a juicer (not a blender!), and voilà! Pour into a large glass, and drink up!

I promise you that it's the yummiest juice you will ever have. My husband and I invested in a good juicer and drink this juice every morning. It's the best vitamin and mineral source available, and you don't even taste "the green" in the juice. This drink literally infuses your body with tons of enzymes, and it keeps your immune system strong all year long. Taking daily supplements and vitamins doesn't even compare. Natalia also explains that by juicing vegetables instead of eating them, we can ingest their quintessential organic water, chlorophyll, and enzymes. There are also enzymes trapped deep inside the fibers of fresh vegetables that we can't absorb through normal digestion but can be released by a juicer.

You can also try other juice combinations, like carrot and apple or beet and pear. Or come up with your own by mixing your favorite fruits and vegetables together. I now buy organic apples and make my own fresh juice whenever I want it. There're no preservatives or sweeteners in homemade juice, so you actually get the real benefits of drinking fruit juice—like all the good-for-you vitamins. I don't buy the bottled grocery store juices anymore. I can't even drink them—because I drink the fresh stuff, that other stuff just tastes gross to me!

Another healthful breakfast option is a big fruit salad with strawberries, bananas, pears, apples, or blueberries. I love to add a touch of agave nectar, which is an all-natural sweetener similar to honey that comes from cactus. Health food stores like Whole Foods usually carry it. Whatever you do, don't use sugar to sweeten your breakfast! If you must add sweetness and can't find agave, try organic honey instead. It's better for you.

EATING LOTS OF FRUIT AND VEGGIES

Mixed greens, fruits, and vegetables that are organic are a must for any healthy eating plan. They're chock-full of vitamins and minerals, and can prevent illness and disease. Antioxidants, which are compounds found in plant food, are known to reduce the risk of cancer, heart attack, and stroke. In terms of being part of a beauty regimen, eating fresh produce is also beneficial for making your hair glossy and keeping your skin clear. Most of my diet is made up of organic fruits and veggies. Although it wasn't always that way. When I was in high school, I loved anything fried, sweet, or greasy. You know, the standard teen fare. One of my faves was Applebee's Chicken Finger Basket with French fries and honey mustard sauce. I think about it sometimes and cringe at how I used to eat.

Making the switch to eating healthfully took a lot of willpower and hard work on my part. Reaching for the carrot sticks instead of the potato chips required diligence and patience. It took a while, but now I know that if I don't eat the healthy stuff, I pay for it later. Either I break out, gain weight, have no energy, or get stomachaches. I'd rather feel good from eating fresh food that's not processed.

Here are some of my favorite recipes. They're simple and amazingly delicious. Remember, try to buy all-organic ingredients.

YUMMY GUACAMOLE

1 Haas avocado

2 tablespoons of minced purple onion

2 tablespoons of diced tomato

a dash of sea salt, pepper, and cayenne pepper to taste

1. Cut the avocado open and spoon out the flesh into a bowl.

2. Mash the avocado and throw in everything else.

3. You can eat this with a toasted sprouted-grain pita (which you can toast in the oven).

TASTY TOMATOES

This recipe takes less than five minutes, and it's a great snack or salad to go with a main course.

1 tomato

extra-virgin olive oil

salt and pepper

basil (if desired)

1. Slice your favorite ripe tomato—I like Romas, heirloom, or the little cherry ones.

2. Drizzle extra-virgin olive oil over the top.

3. Sprinkle with a little salt and pepper.

4. If you happen to have fresh basil, you can chop it up for a garnish.

Here are a couple recipes for vegetables you probably don't like. I didn't either! But I swear when veggies are cooked the right way, they can be delicious.

ROASTED BEETS

You can either eat them hot as a side dish—or let them cool and serve in a salad. They get really tasty when they're roasted, which brings out their sweet flavor, and the extra-virgin olive oil makes them kind of caramelized.

beets

extra-virgin olive oil

salt and pepper

garlic powder

1. Preheat the oven to 400°F.

2. Peel beets (as little or as many as you want) and cut them into chunks. Put chunks in a casserole dish.

3. Drizzle extra-virgin olive oil over the chopped beets.

4. Sprinkle salt, pepper, and garlic powder over them.

5. Bake for about 45 minutes to an hour, or until tender.

BRUSSELS SPROUTS

A lot of people don't like the flavor of these little cabbagelike veggies, because they can be really bitter. But I found a way of cooking them that makes that bitter flavor go *adios*! It's supereasy.

Brussels sprouts

2 tablespoons of extra-virgin olive oil

salt and pepper

1. Wash and trim the ends off the sprouts and peel away any leaves that are funky.

2. Cut the sprouts into quarters. Some of the leaves may fall off—keep those and use them.

3. Heat 2 tablespoons of olive oil in the skillet. Once the pan is hot, add the sprouts and any extra leaves.

4. Add salt and pepper.

5. Cook until the sprouts are tender and starting to caramelize on the outside—they turn crispy and golden brown. This takes about 10 to 12 minutes.

COOL THE CARBS

You've probably heard about lots of celebrities going on "no carb" diets. The problem with this is that our bodies need starches so the "no carb" thing won't last. Here you'll learn that there are plenty of starches out there that are way healthier than those in the typical American diet. Most Americans don't eat enough of the good starches and binge on the bad ones like:

- white flour, which is in white bread, crackers, chips, and pasta
- white rice
- potatoes and French fries

YAMS

They're sooo yummy! When you bake sweet potatoes, as opposed to boiling them, the flavor becomes even sweeter.

1. Poke yams with a fork several times to make little steam holes.
2. Pop them into the oven to bake for about 40 minutes at 350°F (or until they're nice and soft).
3. Let them cool off just a bit.
4. Then scoop out the center and mash it.

IF YOU NORMALLY EAT	SUBSTITUTE WITH
sweets	raw fruit drizzled with agave
white-flour foods	Sprouted-grain breads are the best, but if you can't find them, opt for whole grain breads and crackers.
white rice	If you have to have rice, then try brown rice. You can even order it at most restaurants. I eventually cut it out altogether.
soda, other carbonated drinks, and sugary drinks	Try water with a little lemon, lime, or orange juice squeezed in. Even diet soda isn't good for you.
white potatoes	sweet potatoes, pumpkin, and acorn and butternut squash
French fries	baked sweet-potato fries

These aren't typical starches but our bodies digest them as such:

avocados
legumes
cooked corn

LIMIT DAIRY

I don't eat dairy. Cutting out cheese has been extremely difficult for me, because I used to love putting cheese on everything—or eating it just by itself. But I found some healthy substitutes. Alta Dena raw goat's milk cheese is easier for my body to digest. And I use almond milk in place of regular cow's milk, which has all sorts of hormones and other things that aren't good for us. It's actually mucus forming, and I don't need dairy to get calcium—I get a sufficient daily dose from all the leafy greens in my Green Lemonade.

AVOID THE JUNK FOOD AISLE

Skip items from the chip, cookie, and soda aisle. If you don't have these foods in your house, you won't be tempted to eat them. Reach for an apple or carrot sticks instead when you feel like snacking.

FORGET FAST FOOD

Fast food restaurants are an absolute no-no for me! I admit that I love a burger as much as the next girl. And every once in a while, I do indulge, though only at good restaurants, never drive-thrus. I've done research on the ingredients at a few fast food joints, and discovered a lot of gross and unappetizing stuff. Plus, I'd rather spend the money I'd shell out at Mickey D's on something else.

VITAMINS

We always hear about how good vitamins are for us, and there are always tons of commercials on TV promoting one brand or another. If your eating plan includes juicing and regular doses of fruits and veggies, chances are you don't need to take vitamins. But check with your doctor to see if you should be taking any supplements.

TREAT YOURSELF

Sometimes I crave chocolate cupcakes or ice cream. We all probably have similar cravings. Since most of the time I eat nutritious properly combined food, I do give myself occasional treats. Like I'll go to my favorite bakery (here in LA there's a place called Sprinkles that is THE best) and get one cupcake. I don't bring anything home with me because I know myself all too well. If there's an extra cupcake, I will end up eating it!

NEVER SKIP A MEAL

Don't ever starve yourself. It's not good for your mind, body, or spirit. I've seen plenty of girls at pageants who don't eat so they can fit into their dresses. Instead of doing well at the competition, they often do worse because their blood sugar is all messed up and they can't concentrate. I actually get kind of dizzy if I don't eat—I couldn't imagine walking in heels and a swimsuit if I felt that way. What if I fell? And if I was expected to stay focused in class or at a job? Forget it—not if my stomach's empty.

Now that I'm in Hollywood, I notice this town is crawling with women who think the route to beauty is being rail thin, so they just don't eat. I'm here to tell you, not eating is not right. Starving yourself to be beautiful is not beautiful at all. Instead of choosing not to eat something, you should be a lot more conscious about what you put in your body.

CHANGE THE WAY YOU THINK ABOUT FOOD

Americans have a strange relationship with food—it's what we turn to for comfort and how we celebrate. But we need to think about what we eat in terms of sustenance and how it makes our bodies feel and perform, rather than giving us a quick fix.

If adding more fruits and veggies or cutting out white-flour foods is a totally foreign concept to you, it may be difficult to make the transition at first. You're going to have to change your mind-set about food.

First of all, think about what you *do* eat rather than what you *don't* eat. Then savor each bite. I don't mean to go "Mmmm . . . mmmmm" the whole time, but enjoy your food. Think about what you're eating. Make sure you actually take time to eat. Sit down at the table to eat rather than leaning against the counter and gobbling your meal in two bites. My husband and I sit down to dinner just about every night. Besides it being healthier for us, it's a nice way to catch up and reconnect with each other after a long day.

GET OUT OF A FOOD RUT

It's easy to get bored with food. If you watched the same movie over and over or read the same book again and again, you know you'd get bored. Food is the same way. You've got to keep it interesting. Try new vegetables. Try new recipes. I love poring over the recipes in *The Raw Food Detox Diet* cookbook, and trying out new ways to cook chicken, fish, or broccoli (who knew there were so many things you could do with that green stalk?). The Internet has tons of resources for finding recipes. Also, I find that if I'm the one preparing the dish, I appreciate it even more because I know exactly how much time and energy went into making it. Plus, I know every single ingredient.

Eating healthfully is essential when striving for true beauty. It works both inside and out. Good nutrition can regulate your weight, clear up acne, build stronger bones and muscles, and make you smarter. *¡Buen appetito!*

My older sister struggled with being overweight all her life. At the age of twenty-nine, she finally decided to do something about it and lost ninety pounds over the course of a year. She did it by changing her eating plan, cutting out the bad stuff, and adding more of the good stuff. She also started working out more—something she hadn't been doing enough of before. It was a constant battle for her, but she's kept the weight off for two years!

Snack Pack

I like to keep healthy snacks with me when I know I'm going to be working late or have to travel. My favorite snacks to keep on hand are:

raw carrot sticks
raw almonds
wasabi peas
grapes
Luna Bars (raw snack bars that are delish—you can find them at Whole Foods or other health-food stores)
dried fruit, like mango-and-banana chips mixed with raw nuts

Note: If you can, try to buy organic. Organic products are grown in humane ways and don't use toxic pesticides or other harmful chemicals. They're better for us and the environment!

Get Moving! Exercise

Along with good nutrition, exercise is extremely necessary when it comes to developing inner and outer beauty. Moving your body gets your blood flowing and your mind working. Exercise is probably the most crucial way I've learned to develop confidence.

I'm used to being pretty active. When I wasn't running track or playing volleyball, I did all kinds of other physical activities for fun—like Rollerblading and hiking. I would highly recommend getting involved in some kind of sport at your school or in your community. There are tons of options, like soccer, swimming, tennis, basketball, volleyball, softball, track, dancing, and long-distance running. These types of sports are great for cardiovascular fitness—the exercise that's good for your heart.

Another key part of a balanced exercise plan is strength training, which means lifting weights or resistance training. Yoga is also a form of strength training. This ancient Eastern practice often combines strength training, cardio, and stretching, which makes it a really well-rounded way of working out. It also has a spiritual component, which makes it really appealing to me. You can give thanks during your practice, set intentions, and meditate on your personal mantra.

You don't need to have a trainer to get in shape. Nor do you need to join a gym to get a great workout. Just put on your sneakers and take a walk or jog around the neighborhood. I find running on a treadmill or bouncing up and down on the elliptical machine to be pretty boring anyway. And actually those machines don't get you as fit as running outside does. Running is my go-to workout. You're breathing fresh air and experiencing nature, which is good for the body *and* the soul. There are other workouts you can do on your own that don't require tons of dough. Try Rollerblading, jumping rope, playing basketball with friends, hiking, hula hooping (You can find adult-sized hoops at most sporting-goods stores. This is especially good for trimming waists. And it's fun, too! Sometimes I crack up while I'm doing it because it just feels so silly.), and sit-ups and push-ups (this is a quick exercise you can do in your home).

TRY *These Moves*

Salsa

Dancing is a fun way to get in shape. The salsa is a really popular Latin dance. You often see it in ballroom-dancing competitions. In Los Angeles, New York City, and Miami, there are tons of clubs where people go to show off their moves. But you can learn how to salsa at home. Put on your favorite song and try these steps to the beat.

1. Stand with your feet together.
2. Step forward with your left foot.
3. Rock back onto your right foot.
4. Step your left foot back center.
5. Then step back with your right foot.
6. Rock forward onto your left foot.
7. Return the right foot to center.
8. Repeat, adding your own crazy moves—like waving your arms and overexaggerating your hip movements. This is what my sister and I used to perform for Mami in the kitchen! Like the great salsa legend Celia Cruz used to say, *"AZUCA!"*

Triceps Dips

This is a good one for building the muscles on the backs of your arms. I do dips every single day to keep my arms toned.

1. First sit on the edge of a chair, bench, or step.
2. Place your hands on the edge of the chair, right next to your body, fingers facing forward.
3. Lift your body off the chair, and lower your booty toward the floor, bending your elbows.
4. Push yourself back up by straightening your arms.
5. Do three sets of ten to fifteen reps.

Be sure your back stays straight and your hips stay right under your shoulders.

Yoga Cat Pose

Yoga can help strengthen your body and spirit, and it is such an amazing stress reliever. Here's one of my favorite moves.

1. Start on your hands and knees.
2. Inhale and flex your belly downward as you lift your chin up and look to the sky.
3. Hold for a few counts.
4. Suck in your belly button. Imagine it pulling up so much it can touch your spine.
5. Arch your back like a scary Halloween cat, head down, neck long.
6. Take a breath.
7. Repeat four times.

Pilates Power in Numbers

Pilates works your core muscles—that's the area in the center of your body that helps with good posture, flexibility, and strength. My favorite move is called hundreds. It's called that because you're supposed to do about a hundred of them at a time.

1. Lie on your back with your knees bent.
2. Stretch your arms out by your sides, keeping them straight.
3. Tilt your head forward, keeping your chin down and your gaze toward your tummy.
4. Pump your arms up and down, taking five breaths out and five breaths in.
5. Try to repeat ten times, without bringing your head back to the floor.
6. If you want to make it harder, lift your legs off the ground, extending your feet. You can raise your legs straight up, or try to keep them parallel to the floor.

Learning How to Give Yourself a Break

One of the most important (and my favorite) parts of any health-and-beauty routine is taking the time to pamper yourself—whether it's by having a spa party, getting your nails done at a salon, going for a walk, or sleeping in until noon. Setting aside even just a half hour can be rejuvenating, making you look fresh and well rested.

There are times when I put a lot of pressure on myself, and if I just keep going full steam ahead, I can really start to feel and look worn-down. What I've learned is that you need to be gentle with yourself, and pay attention to when you might be pushing yourself too far. Take a break once in a while. Give yourself a treat. Reward your hard work.

When my volleyball team used to have a big tournament coming up, I would get pretty stressed out, wondering, "Will we win? Will I score enough points? Did I practice hard enough? What if we lose?" I found that if I took a little time for myself before the game, I'd be calmer and more focused.

What do I mean by taking time for yourself? Sometimes we just need a break, a little time to relax from household chores and homework and hobbies and working so hard.

I've also found that you can't be as good a friend, sister, daughter, student, team member, or employee if you don't feel good about yourself.

Treat yourself with love and respect. Don't be any harder on yourself than the way you would treat others.

You can also take time out for yourself by giving yourself a Free Day. My favorite way to spend a Free Day is to rent a few movies and watch them while eating my favorite Ben & Jerry's ice cream, like Oatmeal Cookie Chunk or Chubby Hubby . . . yum! Or during the holidays I treat myself with a Starbucks Pumpkin Spice Latte. When I feel like I still need a treat, but want a healthier option, I'll slice a bunch of strawberries and toss them in a bowl with honey or agave. Honey is really good for you, especially raw honey—it's full of vitamins and is a great boost when you're feeling fatigued. A pot of chamomile or mint tea goes perfectly with the berries.

Think about how you like to unwind. Maybe vegging out in front of the TV, or sleeping in a little bit later, or staying in your PJs all day. If you have plans with friends—like going to see a movie or eating at your favorite restaurant—see if you can choose the flick or the dinner spot that night.

Hair: The Long and Short of It

When I was in fifth grade, I went to our local hairdresser and asked her to give me a mullet—you know, that's the haircut that's short on the top and sides and long in the back? Yeah, yeah . . . go ahead and laugh. But back then everyone in my family had that hairdo—my sister, my cousins—so I thought it was the coolest style ever. Don't ask me why. And it wasn't like I got that cut once and then wised up. Oh, no. I had that same do for years, until I finally got some sense, grew it out, and had a normal haircut again. Looking back, I can recognize it was a pretty bad style that did absolutely nothing to enhance my features.

Like your smile, your hair is one of the first things people notice when they see you. The right hairstyle can create a frame for your face that highlights your best features. And, like fashion, your hairstyle can be an expression of who you are. Think about what your hairstyle might say about you.

Which Do Is Right for You?

Sometimes hairstyles can be challenging, but finding something that works for you is not impossible. To find the right style, first you have to consider the shape of your face. In order to determine your face shape, stand in front of the mirror, pull your hair back, and study your face.

> *Is your jaw square? If so, you have a square face.*
> *Is your forehead wide and your chin narrow? This is a heart-shaped face.*

Is your face long and narrow? You have a long face.

Do you have round cheeks and cherubic features? Your face is round.

Is your face symmetrical at the top and bottom? This is an oval face.

Here are some hairstyles depending on what shape your face is:

SQUARE

Square faces are well complemented with soft, wavy locks that fall just past the jawline. Avoid short cuts and anything too symmetrical because they will make you look hard and severe.

HEART-SHAPED

This shape looks best with styles that add volume to the chin. Chin-length or slightly longer bobs, with ends that flip out are good choices. Side-swept bangs also work well on heart-shaped faces.

LONG

Chin-length cuts with wispy bangs will help soften and shorten a long face. Styles with too much length only make long faces look longer.

ROUND

Layers around the cheekbones are perfect for round faces because they narrow them. Go for graduated bangs on an angle and volume on top, which will add height.

OVAL

Lucky ovals can get away with all styles—long, short, bobs, you name it—they all look good on oval-shaped faces.

I like to flip through magazines and see what hairstyles look good on celebrities. Once you figure out what shape your face is, find pics of celebs who have your same shape and check out what kind of dos they're sporting. When you get your hair cut, bring along the pictures to show your hairdresser.

Getting Over a Bad Do

I've had many a bad haircut—the kind where I left the salon in tears. One of the worst (and most memorable) bad-hair experiences I had was in eighth grade. Our class was having a graduation party, so it was a big deal—it was going to be *the* party of the year. I wanted to look spectacular. Mami bought me the perfect red party dress, and took me to the salon to get my hair done. I wanted a half-up-half-down do, but the stylist had no clue what she was doing. My hair turned into a big pouffy, half-crazy mess! Needless to say, I left the salon in shambles, bawling my eyes out and panicked because my date was picking me up at any minute. As soon I got home, I ran to the bathroom and tried to fix the disaster, combing it out, smoothing it down, and totally restyling it. I was able to fix it in the nick of time—my date arrived just as I sprayed the last lock in place. Luckily everything turned out peachy—I even looked pretty cute, but I was very upset for a while there. Plus I felt bad that Mami had wasted her hard-earned money on something I was able to do better myself!

Getting a bad haircut can be traumatic. But there are ways to deal with it. First, take a deep breath. Remind yourself it's just hair—it will grow out. (Yeah, right. Easier said than done!)

If you really don't like the cut, ask your hairdresser to fix it. Usually they won't charge you to recut a style they didn't get quite right or were confused about what you wanted. If you're pretty sure the stylist isn't skilled enough, find a different hairdresser and ask her to help you out. Get a recommendation from a friend whose hair you love. This isn't an inexpensive option, though, because you're going to pay for two haircuts—the one you don't like and the one to fix what you don't like.

If you're okay with waiting for the cut to grow out, you can camouflage the bad style by wearing your hair back in a ponytail or bun or wearing a hat or scarf over your head.

To Dye or Not to Dye?

I don't recommend dyeing your hair—it can be superhigh maintenance and tends to get pretty expensive. In fact, I never colored my hair until after I won the Miss Massachusetts USA pageant. Even now I keep it simple and only highlight my color with golden honey shades from time to time. If you are interested in experimenting with dyeing your hair, start slow with maybe a few highlights to brighten up your natural color.

One Hundred Strokes a Night—Not

Did you ever hear that you should brush your hair one hundred strokes every night before bed? Maybe your grandmother recommended it, or you saw someone doing it in an old movie or on a TV show. Well, it's totally false. In fact, brushing your hair too much causes breakage and split ends. So put down that brush!

Hair Wear

I usually figure out how I'm going to style my hair based on what outfit I'm going to wear. This is something I learned during my pageant days, and it makes styling supersimple. When I was competing for Miss USA, I picked out my dress first and then decided how to wear my hair second. I have a couple rules I follow for day-to-day dos. If I'm wearing a turtleneck or shirt that has a high neckline or collar, I wear my hair pulled back into a ponytail or bun. Otherwise, if I left my hair down, there'd be too much going on around my face with my curls and the long neck of the outfit. Pulling back your hair makes for a clean, sophisticated look. For V-necks or strapless or spaghetti strap tops, I like to wear my hair down.

It's fun to experiment. Sometimes I blow my hair straight and then use a flat iron to get it really sleek and shiny. Or I'll use hot rollers to add soft curls. I can also part it in the middle and let it cascade over my shoulders. Most days I wear it natural, which is long and curly. Then I put a little gel in it and dry it with a diffuser as I scrunch my hair with my hands.

A diffuser is one of those attachments that fits over the end of a blow dryer. They're made to help dry curly hair without turning it into a big frizz ball. The gel also adds a little shine, which is great because curly hair has a tendency to look dull.

If you have a big event coming up, get your girlfriends together and experiment with one another's hair to find the best style for the occasion. Here are some of my personally recommended options for you to try.

SLEEK BUN

This is my go-to hairdo. I wear my hair back on both good-hair days and those not-so-good-hair days or when I need to style my hair fast. Here's how I do it.

- First, pull your hair back into a ponytail.
- Wrap with an elastic hair band. (Rubber bands pull on your hair, so don't use those!)
- Wrap the ponytail around the elastic band to form the bun.
- Pin in place with bobby pins.
- Then I spray on a little hair spray and comb down any strands that stick up on the side of my head. I want the style to look very smooth.

LOOPED BUN

Another easy do is the looped bun. Here's how you do it:

- Pull your hair back into a ponytail, securing with an elastic band.
- Curl the tail under into a looped roll against your head.
- Pin it with bobby pins.
- Fan the bun out a little so the effect is a wide looped roll.

EASY UP DO

- Pull your hair into a high ponytail with an elastic band.
- Separate hair into sections.
- Twist or curl the sections and secure with bobby pins.
- Experiment with thick and thin sections.
- Spray with hair spray to keep in place.

FRENCH TWIST

This is a classic up do that's very elegant. It looks hard, but it's actually pretty easy to style.

- Pull your hair back and to one side.
- Twist your hair straight up the center of your head.
- Pin it with bobby pins on the inside of the twist.
- There will likely be a little puff of extra hair at the top of the twist. Take this end and twist it back into the roll, pinning it in place.
- Finish with hair spray to smooth out the sides.

HALF-UP DO

- Lift the top section of your hair straight up.
- Back comb or "tease" it. This means to comb the back part of your hair toward your roots. It will make it look a little frizzy, but this trick adds some nice texture.
- Smooth the top of this section to tame the frizz, without getting rid of the lift.
- Pull the section back from your temples, leaving length in back.
- Secure with a hair clip.

CASCADING CURLS

I like to call this Victoria's Secret Hair, because it ends up looking sexy like the models in the catalog. It's a style that I reserve for special occasions, because it takes so long to do. It's great for a red carpet look though. I love it and I think you'll like it, too! With practice, this style will save you from having to spend all kinds of dough at the salon. And you can recruit a friend to help you out. Here's how I do it:

- First I apply a hair-straightening balm to my hair, then blow it out using a round brush. I dry it in sections so the hair becomes as smooth as possible.
- Once it's all blown out, I take sections, spray a little Redken Spray Starch on the section of hair, and roll it up in a hot roller. This Redken product helps to hold the curl better. I continue until all the hair is up in the rollers.
- Let the rollers cool completely (I like to do my makeup at this point because my hair is out of my face) before removing them. I finish by running my fingers through my hair and spraying a little hair spray to keep the curls in place. You can also tease some hair at the crown of your head for added volume and part your hair for a more styled look.

The Right Products

Like selecting the right hairstyle, choosing the right hair products takes some trial and error. I've learned that the best way to figure out which products work for my hair is to try them—and then keep trying until I find stuff I like. One product I can't live without is Bio Silk Glazing Gel. If you have curly hair, I highly recommend you try it.

MAKEUP

Learning how to wear makeup was one of the most useful skills I gained back in my early modeling and pageant days. When I went on modeling auditions, or go-sees, I wore very little makeup so the casting directors could really see my features and know what they had to work with. At pageants, on the other hand, I was rarely without makeup, and I don't think I saw the other girls without makeup, either. Even though we were supposed to look young and sweet, makeup is a pageant-world staple: foundation, concealer, lipstick, eyeliner, mascara, even fake eyelashes!

As I moved away from the pageant world, I learned how to wear makeup for more real-world situations. Now I have a few different makeup routines, depending on where I'm going and what time of day it is. Usually for everyday makeup, I keep it light and natural. If I have an audition or I am just hanging out, I don't want to be covered up by tons of foundation and eye shadow. Plus, wearing too much makeup can often make you appear older than you are. I think it's important to look young, fresh, and your age.

If I'm going out to dinner with friends or to a Hollywood soiree, I like to wear makeup that's a bit more dramatic. My nighttime regimen usually includes more color, a little shimmer, and dark eyeliner.

Something that I would recommend, if you haven't already, is to invest in a set of makeup brushes. Well-made brushes can make a big difference in the application of makeup. They will help you achieve a more smooth, well-blended finish.

Purchasing a set can get expensive, but you'll have them for a long time if you properly care for them.

SMOKY EYES

Smoky eyes give anyone a glam look. Here's how to do it. Practice on your friends!

Use dark brown, navy, gray, or dark purple eye shadows. Dab your lids with concealer or foundation. This sets a nice base for the shadow and will help keep it in place. You can also use what's called an eye-shadow primer. Next, apply eyeliner to the top lid, just above the lash line. Make the line thicker in the middle. Ideally you want your liner to match your shadow, so if you're using dark brown shadow, use dark brown liner. But if you don't have stuff that matches exactly—no worries! You can still achieve the effect you want. On your bottom lid, apply a lighter streak of liner and smudge it. Now you're ready for the shadow! Use a light shimmery color to start and apply this to your entire lid and brow bone. Then apply the darker color, but just on your lid. I like to start from the outer edges of my lids and work in so it blends nicely. You can add a bit of the shadow to your lower lid for even more of the smudged look. Top it all off with several coats of mascara.

TEN-MINUTES-A-DAY MAKEUP ROUTINE

Some days you just don't have much time to get ready. I like to be as low maintenance as possible, so I've worked out a no-fail plan for getting it together in next to no time.

After you've jumped out of the shower and your hair is wet, wrap it up in a towel. Then dab a little concealer under your eyes and on any blemishes. Pad the concealer with your finger—it's really important to blend. I add a little blush to the apples of my cheeks—blush adds a nice hint of color. Then I slick on just a touch of mascara to bring out my eyes. I finish with a lip gloss or moisturizer with SPF on my lips for a really natural day look. Neutrogena has some great affordable ones like the MoistureShine Soothing LipSheers. My favorite color is Cool Nectar, because it just enhances my natural lip color. Now I'm ready for my hair. Since I have curly locks, I use a diffuser to dry, and it only takes ten minutes. If you have straight hair, you can dry your hair as you normally do. Once it's dry, I leave it down, clip it back for a half-up-half-down look, or pull it back into a ponytail, hair spray any bits that are sticking out, and I'm ready to go!

MAKEUP BAG MUSTS

There are a few items I never leave home without:

> *Lip moisturizer (I have it with me at all times!)*
> *M·A·C lip gloss*
> *Neutrogena Mineral Sheers Blush (This is so cool. It's blush with a built-in brush. There's a cap on it, so it won't make a mess in your purse. Great for those midday touchups!)*
> *Hair elastic, if my hair is down*

Eyebrow Know-How: Leave Them to a Professional

Having neatly trimmed eyebrows can make a huge difference in your appearance. Properly shaped brows lift the eyes and make them appear more open. They can change the whole look of your face. But they have to be done right; otherwise you can end up looking ridiculous, which happened to me.

When I was fourteen years old and a freshman in high school, my cousin Betsy said that she wanted to pluck my eyebrows for me. I had never plucked them and thought it sounded like such a grown-up thing to do, so excitedly I said, "Yes!" Betsy was sixteen and by no means a professional eyebrow shaper. I don't know why I let her touch mine. I think I was just excited—plucking my eyebrows seemed like some kind of rite of passage toward adulthood. Plus, I thought that Betsy knew what she was doing. Well, she ended up overplucking my eyebrows and making them way too thin. But I wore them like that all through high school.

Then in college I decided I wanted a more natural look. I went to a brow specialist, who told me not to touch them and just let them grow for a while. Once they'd come back in, she'd reshape them. Oh my God, was that a crazy time! The hair grew in in clumps—it looked really weird. I noticed that it wasn't growing in a couple of places so I had bald spots on my eyebrows. I was horrified! I had to walk around college and go to class like this! I would wear hats to disguise my fuzzy, unplucked eyebrows. I even have photos of me at this senior-year event that I absolutely hate because of my eyebrows. When I asked the specialist about the bald spots, she said that sometimes, when someone's been plucking for many years, the hair follicle can die, and the hair in that area might never grow back. Well, it looked like I had a bunch of dead follicles. I even tried putting Rogaine on them—you know, that stuff for bald men! Nothing worked. Still to this day, I have to fill in the bald spots in my eyebrows with a brow pencil. Bummer!

So the moral of my story is . . . don't ever let ANYONE, except a professional, shape your eyebrows!

I know that some people pluck their brows themselves,

and I've seen special brow-shaping tools at the drugstore. But I recommend that you don't try to do it yourself. It's just too easy to mess up. Your eyes are the window to your soul. It's the first thing that people see when they meet you. Your eyebrows frame your eyes, so their shape is super important.

Seeing a professional brow shaper is worth the money—it usually costs around fifteen to twenty dollars at most salons, and I'm telling you that it's well worth the money. Make sure to ask the specialist questions and find out how long they have been doing eyebrows. It's totally fine to ask for photos of clients so you can see their work. I think that your best bet is to do a little research on the Internet and find out who's the best in your area. If you live outside a major city, I would find someone in the city, since there are usually more experienced hairstylists, makeup artists, and brow specialists there.

Skin Care

Skin is the largest organ in the human body. It protects us—and can also drive us nuts! You might be experiencing all kinds of frustrating skin freak-outs. It's totally normal for your skin to break out, get oilier, and change texture as you get older. But there are some things you can do to help your skin stay bright and glowing.

First of all, what you eat and drink affects your skin. Lots of water and good nutrition make all the difference in your skin. Too much caffeine and alcohol tend to prematurely age the skin and can lead to broken blood vessels, big pores, and other unwanted blemishes. We really are what we eat.

If you tend to have oily skin with frequent breakouts, steer clear of foundations that are oil-based. They'll clog your pores. Tinted moisturizers are great and my personal favorite. And if you aren't going anywhere special, give your face a break and don't wear any makeup.

Wash your face twice a day, when you wake up in the morning and just before bed. My favorite face wash is Neutrogena Iluminating Microderm Cleansing Pads, because they wash your face and exfoliate dead skin at the same time. Be careful not to wash your face too much, though, as you can dry out your dermis. And take care to be gentle—scrubbing too hard can aggravate sensitive or broken-out skin. If you have sensitive skin, like me, you can try a non-soap-based cleanser. I find they can be much gentler on my skin.

Wear sunscreen! If you're outside a lot or live in a warm climate, sunscreen is essential every single day. It will protect you from dangerous UV rays and will also keep your skin looking younger longer. Try to buy brands with at least thirty SPF for maximum protection. Look for moisturizers with sunscreen, which are great for keeping skin dewy. Neutrogena's Healthy Defense Daily Moisturizer is one of my staples.

If you have pimples, don't pick them! I know it's hard not to, but picking can make them get bigger or even become infected. I like to use Clearasil pads after I wash my face to help clear up my skin, but only when I have a breakout because it dries out my skin. Another great pimple fighter—one that's totally natural—is aloe vera gel. A little dab will usually dry up zits overnight. Aloe vera also takes away the sting or pain of a big pimple and reduces redness, swelling, and excess oil production. Plus, it's really inexpensive and can be found at most drugstores.

Tea tree oil is another natural remedy. I add a drop of the antiseptic to my moisturizer and apply it to my face when I have a pimple. It helps kill the bacteria that can cause blemishes.

I'm also a stickler about washing my sheets—especially

pillowcases—once or twice a week. There is so much dirt and oil clinging to your pillowcase from your skin and your hair, and you probably don't even notice! This residue can cause pimples, too, so make sure that your bedsheets are always clean and change them at least once a week.

Homemade Beauty Treatments

Here are recipes for some of my favorite at-home beauty remedies. They're as luxe as what you'll find at any spa—but a lot cheaper because they're made with ingredients you probably already have in your pantry. You can use these recipes to pamper yourself—or share them with friends at the Show Your Appreciation Spa Party mentioned in Key #2.

Note: If you're allergic to any of these ingredients, don't use the recipe! I don't want you to break out or have to take a trip to the hospital.

BROWN SUGAR SCRUB

Scrubs are good for exfoliating your skin and leaving it soft and supple. You can use this scrub on your whole body, but don't use it if your skin is really broken out—it could irritate your blemishes.

- Mix one cup brown sugar with a half cup of extra-virgin olive oil or coconut oil.
- Gently rub a small amount into skin, working it in slowly.
- You can also use in the shower if you want to give your bod a scrub down.
- Gently rinse off with warm water.

SKIN SMOOTHER

Supereasy. Just rub some olive oil into your skin. I like to use it on places that get really dry, like elbows and knees.

ROSEMARY STEAM

Steams are great for opening pores and getting your skin ready for masks and other treatments.

- Boil a pot of water.
- Add sprigs of fresh rosemary and lavender (you can find these herbs at most local grocery stores in the produce section).
- Let the water continue to boil for a few minutes so the herbs steep.
- Pull your hair back.
- Turn off the boiling water, but make sure steam is still rising from it.
- Lean over the pot (but not too close) with a hand towel over the back of your head, forming a tent.
- Let the steam permeate your skin.

GOOD-BYE, PUFFY EYES

There are a couple of home remedies for reducing under-eye puffiness.

Slice a chilled cucumber. Place slices over your eyes for five to ten minutes. You will have to lie down to do this.

You can also use a couple of teabags. Rinse two teabags with cold water and place in the freezer to chill. Once chilled, place over eyes for five to ten minutes.

ROSE PETAL FOOT SOAK

This is really easy, especially if you or any of your friends have rosebushes. Fill a bucket or foot soaker with warm or hot water. Add rose petals. Rest your feet in the water and relax.

Whatcha Gonna Wear?

I have to be really conscious of what I wear at all times, because I'm often in the spotlight, whether I'm on the red carpet or on television. I didn't always know how to choose the right outfit—it's another one of those things I had to learn, which is why I know you can learn what to wear, too.

Believe it or not, what you wear does say something about you—whether you're the kind of girl who's always rockin' the latest trends or you're more of a jeans and T-shirt kind of gal. Here's a funny story about what kind of impression we give by what we choose to wear. I have a friend whose dad is an actor. He once had a role playing a cop. During a break, he went off set to grab coffee when a woman in trouble ran over to him and yelled, "Officer, please help! A man stole my purse!" He was still in his uniform! (Which was actually his costume.) Since he wasn't a cop, he couldn't actually *do* anything except tell the poor woman to go to the police station down the street. What you wear communicates a message to people, even when you don't mean to. Your "uniform" can speak volumes about who you are to others. You want to convey to them that you've got it together. Wearing the right outfit is all about looking effortless—even if it took you hours to create that look!

I've found it's helpful to develop a signature style. Great style is all about personal power. What does that mean? It's kind of like creating your own fashion playbook by figuring out what style you most identify with and what cuts look good on you. Once you know what your style is, creating an outfit or going shopping becomes a no-brainer because you have an array of go-to shapes, colors, fabrics, and styles that make dressing room drama disappear.

Developing your own personal style will also help you acquire what I like to call "a fashion instinct"—trusting your intuition about what looks best on you. When I was working as a VJ at MTV, I had a great stylist who helped me choose what to wear on the show. Every once in a while, she picked an outfit that she thought was perfect for me, but I wasn't feeling it. I wore her choices anyway because I thought she knew best—she was the stylist, after all. But I noticed on those days we didn't agree on my attire, I was overconcerned about how I looked and, as a result, didn't do as well hosting the show. From those experiences, I learned to trust my gut and wear outfits that made *me* feel great.

So how do you figure out your style? Think about what looks good on you. What styles do you like to wear? What do you want people to read from what you wear? What style represents who you are? Too confusing? Take the following quiz to help figure out your inner fashionista.

What's Your Style?

1. **You'd describe yourself as:**
    a. a jock
    b. feminine
    c. traditional
    d. curious
    e. a wild child

2. **Your fave weekend outfit is:**

   a. sweatpants and a tank top

   b. Weekend outfit? You wear the same thing on weekends as you do during the week: skirt and blouse, hair done, lip gloss on.

   c. jeans and a blazer

   d. You don't have a favorite—you like to mix it up and try new styles.

   e. Bright colors, plaids and other prints—you never know when your BFF might call with tickets to a No Doubt concert.

3. **You want to dress to impress. You wear:**

   a. an awesome new pair of sneaks and your favorite team's jersey

   b. a dress with fluttery sleeves in a flirty pastel color

   c. a secretary top, pencil skirt, and pumps

   d. whatever outfit is on this month's cover of *Lucky Magazine*

   e. skinny black jeans, a vintage cropped jacket, and ankle boots, plus lots of bangle bracelets and a dangly pendant necklace

4. **You want to get that hot guy to notice you, so you:**

   a. free throw your math notes into the trash can

   b. bat your eyelashes and smile coyly whenever he looks your way

   c. ask him if he's ever read Ayn Rand

   d. tell him you like his shirt

   e. wear your White Stripes concert tee and hope he comments on it

5. **You're going to be spending the whole summer at the beach on a family vacation. You pack:**

   a. shorts, sweats, tank tops, T-shirts, jeans, sweatshirts . . . did I already say "sweats"?

b. cotton sundresses, sparkly sandals, your bikini, and a sarong

c. capris and superstylin' sunglasses

d. everything in your closet—you never know what you might need!

e. a variety—everything from vintage hoop earrings to your fave one-piece bathing suit to this season's latest shorts

Mostly As: Sporty

You'd rather be playing ball than fussing over what to wear. Your style is all about being comfy and casual. Just make sure you don't wear torn sweatpants or stinky gym shoes. Just because your clothes are comfy doesn't mean they should be sloppy. Yoga pants, instead of sweatpants, or a cute Juicy Couture outfit can be sleek alternatives.

Mostly Bs: Femme Fatale

You love to show off your feminine side. Chances are your wardrobe is full of dresses and skirts in a wide variety of soft colors, like pale pinks, blues, yellows, and greens. Try mixing up your girly style with high-waisted trousers, and pair them with your favorite ruffled top.

Mostly Cs: Sophisticated

You have a traditional sense of style and go for classic items with a more tailored look and neutral color palette—like navy, tan, cream, gray, brown, and black. Just don't get stuck in a color rut. Add touches of color with a bright top, red belt, or gold accessories.

Mostly Ds: Fashion Plate

You have subscriptions to every fashion magazine and love trying out the latest styles. If shopping were a sport, you'd be an Olympic gold medalist! Just don't get too caught up in trends. It's great to be in the know when it comes to fashion, but you want to look like you have your own style—not like you're copying the mannequins in the department store at the mall.

Mostly Es: A Style of Your Own

You definitely dress to the beat of your inner designer. You love mixing all eras and styles and have a knack for finding fun vintage pieces. To you, fashion is all about experimentation and expression—it's an adventure! Just be careful when wearing clothes that are too vintage or too punk or too Goth—you don't want to look like you're wearing a costume so balance it out.

Once you have a basic idea of your signature style, it's important to know what works for you. Just because something is "in" doesn't necessarily mean it'll look good on you. That's okay! It's better to create your own style and wear things that flatter you rather than to always try to follow trends. Trying to keep up with changing trends is exhausting—believe me, I've tried! It's also hard on your pocketbook. Buying a whole new wardrobe each season is expensive and totally unnecessary. I've found that all I need in order to have a well-rounded wardrobe is some key pieces that are timeless.

THE BASICS

Every girl's wardrobe should have these basic items:

- a little black dress
- a pair of casual jeans
- a pair of dressy jeans
- a pair of wide-leg trousers
- a dressy blouse
- a white button-up oxford shirt
- a button-up cardigan sweater in a classic color like black, navy, brown, or beige
- a turtleneck

- a V-neck sweater
- a blazer
- a pencil skirt
- a good coat
- lots of tees and tank tops for layering

Once you have the basics, you can add accessories that highlight your personal style or reflect current trends. Things like belts, scarves, jewelry, tights, glasses, hats, and shoes can take a look from so-so to spectacular.

Slimming Secrets

Everyone wants to know what to wear to look slim. Because I'm often on television—which does add poundage by the way . . . all those rumors about TV adding five pounds are true!—I've learned what to wear to make me look lean on camera.

DARK COLORS

Go for shades like navy, chocolate, brown, or black. Dark colors can make anyone look trim. If you happen to be bigger on the bottom, I would pair dark bottoms with a light top to balance your shape.

VERTICAL STRIPES

We all know horizontal stripes can make you look wider than you are, so stay away! However, *vertical* stripes make you look tall. Look for wide stripes and pinstripes on skirts, dresses, pants, and even tops, vests, and jackets.

WAISTED

I love items that are nipped-in at the waist. A trim waist-line gives the appearance of an hourglass figure. Go for jackets that have a waistband, or are cinched in. Or you can add a belt. When I hosted *Total Request Live*, I loved wearing big belts high on my waistline. They really enhance your shape.

GO-TO STYLE

We all have those days when we're feeling a little, well, "thicker" than usual. Okay, let me be blunt. You know, those "fat days" when nothing seems to fit right. I have an outfit I wear on days like those: a pair of stretchy black corduroys that are supercomfy as well as stylish, a dressy black shirt, and heels. Even if I'm not feeling fab, I look it! Figure out your own go-to outfit and keep it on hand for those "special" days. And, no, I don't mean sweatpants. Those should only be worn if you're going to practice or the gym.

Shape Up

To help me discover my signature style, I had to determine my body type. There are four basic shapes. Most people fit into one or the other, although some people are a combination of body types. Other things to keep in mind when looking for the right fit are height (are you tall or petite?) and weight (are you thin or plus-sized?). There are specific cuts and styles that look particularly good (or bad) on each body type. Here are the four most common shapes:

HOURGLASS

Girls with hourglass figures are the same size on top as on the bottom with small waists. I'm a tall hourglass.

SPOON, OR PEAR-SHAPED

Spoon-shaped girls are bigger on the bottom than on top. They usually have wide hips and a small waist, bust, and shoulders. Think J. Lo and Beyoncé.

TRIANGLE, OR APPLE

If you have a triangle or apple shape, you're big on top and small on the bottom, usually with a big chest and skinny legs. Famous apples include Catherine Zeta-Jones and Elizabeth Hurley.

RECTANGLE, OR RULER

Rectangles are usually long and lean, with not much waist definition. Classic movie goddess Audrey Hepburn is a perfect example of a rectangle.

Your Best Bets

Here are a few examples of what to wear for each body type, but remember that not everyone fits into one "norm." You might fit into two types. So use my suggestions as a starting-off point, but feel free to try different pieces to see what you like best and feel most comfortable in.

BEST STYLES FOR HOURGLASS SHAPES

Wear coats that cinch at the waist to highlight your tiny waist.

Slip on straight-leg pants or jeans that zip on the side. Try a boot-cut style or pants that are slightly flared at the bottom, which will elongate your shape.

Choose dresses that skim (rather than cling) and are cinched at the waist, like wrap dresses, shifts, and dresses with belts.

Go for flat-front skirts that zip on the side or back. A-lines, wraps, and high-waisted pencil skirts show off your femme fatale shape.

Wrap-style tops with deep V-necks work well on hourglasses because they show off their bust and waist.

BEST STYLES FOR SPOONS

Get warm in coats with rounded shoulders and A-line cuts that flare below the waist.

Opt for slightly wider-leg trousers and jeans—they keep a spoon from looking bottom heavy. Go easy on the detailing, though, to curb unwanted attention to hips and legs.

Dresses with A-line skirts, fitted bodices, and Empire waists show off pear-shaped figures.

Try knee-length—or just below the knee—skirts and A-lines.

Match shoes and hose to the color of your skirt or dress—it makes spoons look slimmer.

Balance wide hips and narrow shoulders by wearing blouses with slight shoulder pads, gathered sleeves, and wide collars.

BEST STYLES FOR TRIANGLES

Cozy up in single-breasted coat styles. Avoid military, mandarin, and other high-necked collars.

V-neck dresses elongate a triangle's neckline, while dark colors even out the top and bottom.

Buy classic, simple skirt cuts with a flat front in either A-line or pencil styles.

Avoid pockets or anything that might add bulk.

Stick with tops that have very tailored or narrow collars.

BEST STYLES FOR RECTANGLES

Round out a boyish bod by wearing tailored styles. Consider adding a belt to create a waist.

Look for sport-tailored men's-cut jeans and trousers. Steer clear of anything that's too fitted, as it may create a boxy shape.

Create curves with dresses that have well-defined waistlines, like wrap dresses or belted styles.

Pencil skirts add plenty of curves and swerves.

Because rectangles tend to have flatter chests, wear tops that have embellishment or details like ruching, pleats, and ruffled collars to accentuate what's there.

It's Just a Number

Too often we get hung up on what size we wear. Or we obsess about what size we *aren't*. But you know what? It doesn't matter. Size is just a number. When finding the right clothes, it's all about fit and comfort. What fits you best? Sometimes my size is all over the place. I might be one size at a certain store or in one designer's clothes and a different size in another. Every store, designer and manufacturer sizes clothes differently. A size eight at Target might be a size six at Macy's. You just have to try everything on and see what's most flattering to your figure.

Shoes

When I was in high school, I had quite a collection of sneakers because that's the kind of shoe I wore most often. Once I started modeling and competing in pageants, however, I had to stock my closet with more "girlie" shoes. What I found then was that, like a lot of women, I have a passion for shoes. Love them, love them, love them!

An easy way to dress an outfit up or down is simply by changing your shoes. You can easily take an outfit from day to night by swapping out your ballet flats or sneaks for boots or heels.

Every girl should have a few different styles of shoes in her closet. (Yeah, I mean more than four different pairs of tennis shoes!)

- a pair of comfy flats for everyday wear
- casual sneakers
- tennis shoes you actually work out in
- short heels or dressy flats that you can wear with dresses and to fancy occasions
- boots, either tall or short, that can double as your winter shoes—these look so stylish when you tuck a pair of skinny jeans into them
- sandals (flip-flops don't count—they're too casual)

A little trick I learned from my stylist at MTV was that when you wear a dress with a pair of nude-colored shoes, it makes your legs look longer. It absolutely works, so I suggest you find a pair with a classic style like a Mary Jane.

Hey, you! Once your sneaks have holes or are worn-out, toss 'em! No matter how comfortable they are, there's no excuse for continuing to wear stinky old tennis shoes!

Walk the Runway

Nervous about sporting heels? I was, too. And I had to wear them to walk across the stage in a bathing suit! In order to be able to do that, I had to practice, practice, practice. I spent hours marching around our apartment in pumps and even took lessons from my pageant coaches. If you want to gracefully master walking in heels, I would suggest starting with one-inchers first and then work your way up to higher heels. Practice walking around the house, and even in the backyard, so you get used to walking on different surfaces. Once you feel comfortable, try carrying a full glass of water as you strut. If you can do that, you've become a high heel pro!

Warning: don't wear heels that are too high for you. I never go above two or three inches. Anything higher makes it difficult for me to balance and puts pressure on my arches and my back. Never wear a shoe that doesn't fit well or feel comfortable. If that means you wear flats instead of heels, that's okay! It's better than being in pain.

Get Organized

I like to organize my shoes and my clothes by style so that I have a casual section and a dressy section. Then I organize by color within each section. I've found this method makes getting dressed much easier.

Accessorize

The most fun part about putting together an outfit is accessorizing. It's how you can make an outfit uniquely yours. Three accessories I love to use to finish off an outfit are big bracelets, long necklaces, and classic silver hoops, which go with almost every outfit. (If I'm going to an interview, however, I keep the jewelry to a minimum.)

I also have five big supersoft pashmina-style scarves in different colors that I wear pretty much EVERYWHERE. I can throw them over jeans, nice trousers, or even formal dresses. I love them because they add a little flair to my outfit—and they keep me snuggly and warm.

Style NO-NOS

- Don't wear clothes that don't fit you well—whether too tight or too big. They won't be comfortable or flattering.
- Don't wear any trends that do not look good on you.
- Don't wear clothes that you constantly have to adjust and readjust. You'll never feel confident in an outfit that you're constantly fixing.
- Don't buy an outfit based on the size on the label—buy it based on how well it fits you.

What's Your Color?

No matter how great a cut or style of clothing might look on you, no one will even notice if you're wearing a color that's all wrong for your skin tone. Having a color palette to turn to makes shopping a breeze because you can head straight to your shades. I got my colors done when I was competing in Miss Teen Massachusetts. Turns out, I look good in royal blue, purple, red, and shades of brown and gold.

There's a supersimple way to figure out your colors. This is something you could even do with girlfriends at your spa party.

WHAT YOU NEED:

Three pieces of construction paper: one red, one yellow and one blue.

WHAT YOU DO:

Look at yourself in the mirror. Hold each piece of colored paper up to your face in turn. Which one blends nicely with your skin tone? Which one makes your skin look harsh?

If red looks best, you've probably got red undertones.

If yellow seems to match, your complexion is probably on the olive side with yellow undertones.

If it's blue, you probably have blue undertones.

Red undertones should go for a muted palette of soft colors, like navy, cream, pale yellow, brown, light blue, moss, light peach and beige.

Yellow undertones should choose earthy, vibrant colors like rust, olive green, rich orange, soil brown, and amethyst.

Blue undertones can wear deep, bright colors like royal blue, crimson red, white, turquoise, and forest green.

I always recommend that you just go to a store and try different colored shirts on as well. There may be a color that you just love when you put it on!

Clothes for Any Occasion

Learning what to wear for specific situations was probably the biggest lesson I had to learn. Putting together the right outfit for school, work, a job interview, an audition, or a party or other event can be intimidating. But if you have the right pieces in your wardrobe, pulling together a look can be a snap.

FOR EVERY DAY

Try these on for size:

- wide-leg trousers or jeans
- boot-cut jeans
- A-line and pencil skirts
- T-shirts in different colors and neck shapes (crew, scoop, V-neck, etc.)
- tank tops layered under sweaters or tees
- sundresses with sweaters or shrugs over them
- crisp and fitted button-down shirts
- ballet or other flats
- Vans, Pumas, or other casual sneakers
- blazers, jackets, or wraps (great over tanks or tees with jeans)

To help save time—and stress!—in the morning, choose your outfit the night before.

ACE THE INTERVIEW

Do you have a college, job, or internship interview coming up? You can dress professionally and still look young and stylish. Here are some outfits I suggest:

- flare-leg trousers and ruffle top
- pencil skirt and button-up shirt
- wide-leg pants, vest, and turtleneck
- sailor pants and V-neck sweater
- plain tank with a blazer over it and A-line skirt

PARTY TIME

If you're going to a formal event, a knee-length dress with heels is always a good bet. If it's more casual, a sundress and sandals are perfect in warm weather, while a corduroy skirt, tights, sweater and boots work for winter.

DRESSING FOR A DATE

For dates I recommend a feminine but not-too-revealing look that's both flattering and casual. You don't want to overwhelm your date by overdressing or wearing something that's too formal, so go for jeans and maybe a tee and blazer. Or a comfy sweater and wide-leg trousers. In terms of tops, don't wear anything that reveals too much cleavage! You'll be sending out the wrong message to your date. The three words to keep in mind when choosing a date outfit are casual, fun, and classy.

HANGING WITH THE GIRLS

Unless we're going out somewhere special, I like to be totally me when I'm hanging with my girls. My outfit of choice would be jeans, a cute T-shirt, and casual sneakers, like Vans slip-ons. But even though I'm going casual, I still look nice and put together. Just because I'm hanging out doesn't mean I want to look scruffy.

A GOOD BRA CAN BE YOUR BEST FRIEND

Having the right bra is probably the most important staple in any girl's wardrobe—and it doesn't matter if you're an A or a triple D. Bras can lift, shape, support, and create cleavage no matter what size you are. The wrong bra can pinch, pull, sag, and give you an unwanted look. Have you ever seen women who look like they have a sausage across their chests? Or have four boobs instead of two? The right bra can lift and separate your chest, giving you optimum boobage! LOL!

So how do you find the right size? You can go to any department store's lingerie department, like Macy's, Nordstrom, or even better, check out Victoria's Secret, because it's what they specialize in, and ask someone to fit you for a bra. I used to work at Victoria's Secret, and we would do this all the time. Or you can do it yourself. Here's how.

> *Using a tape measure, measure the area around your rib cage, just under your bust.*
> *Add five inches to the number.*
> *Round up if the number is odd.*
> *Then loosely measure around the fullest part of your bust.*
> *Subtract that number from the measurement of your rib cage to determine your cup size.*

If the number is:

> *1 inch, you're an A.*
> *2 inches, you're a B.*

3 inches, you're a C.

4 inches, you're a D.

5 inches, you're a DD.

6 inches, you're a DDD—wowza, sista!

It's important to always try on bras because each manufacturer sizes them a little bit differently.

WHAT'S *Under There?*

Always make sure you wear underwear!—especially under skirts and dresses! Be a lady. My favorite undies are the boy shorts from Victoria's Secret. They are comfy and thin, so you don't see a panty line easily under clothing. Plus, they come in many fun colors and prints.

FLESHED *Out*

I learned this when I worked at Victoria's Secret. Every girl should have a bra and pair of flesh-colored undies as a staple in her wardrobe. When you wear white clothing, you want to wear flesh-colored undergarments so they blend in with your skin tone. White under white just looks more white!

Great Style Doesn't Have to Break the Bank

You don't have to spend a mint to look like a million bucks. Stores like Wal-Mart, Kohl's, and Target (my fav) offer affordable styles, often by big-name designers. They're great places to stock up on staple items as well as score trendy accessories—and you won't go broke.

Another great place to find great deals on clothes is vintage and thrift stores or consignment shops. You can often find designer pieces that are barely worn. Just make sure they don't have any tears or stains. eBay is another resource—if you like a particular designer you can try on his or her pieces at the mall, and then check on eBay to see if someone is selling them for less. You can often save a bundle this way. Ooo, and let's not forget outlet stores! OMG, I have scored the best stuff at designer shopping outlets that would have cost me a small fortune at normal retail shops. I have a rule that unless I absolutely love something, I will not pay full price for it. If you wait, it will go on sale, or I will shop around for the best price. Outlet stores and sample sales offer savings galore. Outlet malls often have close-outs of big-name designers for cheap. This is another great way to stock up on essentials. If you happen to live near a big city, look online for sample sales in your community. Sample sales are where designers sell their sample designs and overstock items for tons less than retail. Where I live in LA, there's a sample sale nearly every weekend. You can often find items for up to 90 percent off retail and some designers even have five-dollar bins.

Swap Meet 'n' Greet

Organize a clothing swap with your pals. Have everyone bring items they no longer want so you can all trade. This is a fun, free way to get some new duds. Plus, you can clean out your own closet at the same time. It's like a party—with free clothes!

BEHIND-THE-SCENES

Fashion Fixes

These are some useful—and funny!—tricks I learned during my Miss USA and *TRL* days.

Butt Glue

Seriously, this is what they call it in the pageant world. It's used to glue your swimsuit bottoms to your butt so it won't creep up while you're walking across the stage during the swimsuit competition. Even Mami noticed the girls who didn't use it, and pointed out their wedgies. You can also use butt glue to keep a strap from slipping, but use it sparingly because it can get kind of messy and gross! You can find it online—just do a Google search for butt glue. (Really!)

Toupee Tape

Another great tool I learned about during those crazy pageant days is toupee tape strips. They're pieces of double-sided tape usually used to keep hair pieces in place on men. But they work great on the inside of low-cut shirts to keep your bra from showing, prevent a top from falling off your shoulder, or keep a wrap dress secure, etc. . . . The possibilities are endless with this little trick of the trade! I'm always stocked with a packet of toupee tape because it comes in handy more often than not. I used it all the time when I hosted *TRL.*

Chicken Cutlets, aka a Girl's Best Friend

Ah yes, another little somethin' I learned from my pageant days. I don't know why people get boob jobs when these are on the market! Chicken cutlets are actually flesh-toned bust enhancers. You slip them in your bra, and they work great for filling out evening gowns when you need a little extra help on top.

Style Screwups

We've all been there. You thought you were wearing the most awesome outfit *ever*, but when you got to the party, everyone was looking at you sideways.

If you're ever in a situation where you hate your look and can't fix it, you're going to have to play it off. Wear a big giant smile and act like you're totally fine with what you're wearing. "Don't you know, this is the latest trend—it was in *Vogue*." If anyone teases you, come back with "Wait—I thought this was a costume party" or "You mean, it's not Halloween?"

When you're able to laugh at yourself, chances are other people will admire your spunk and forget about your fashion faux pas.

Loving Your Look

Now you know all my secrets for looking great on the outside. Taking a little extra time each day to make yourself look your best goes a long way toward building both your inner and outer beauty. It's so important to put your best foot forward on everything you attempt and what you wear is important, too. It makes for a great first impression and shows that you put care into your appearance. But no matter how beautiful you are on the outside, if you don't feel the same on the inside, others won't see it. Taking control of your health and body image means being in charge of how you *feel* about how you look, too.

You have to love yourself and how you look, beauty marks, warts, and all. If you don't love yourself, how can you expect others to? Loving yourself and how you look will contribute to your confidence, boost self-esteem, and make you a happier person.

I know that it's easy to obsess about certain body parts. You don't like your butt, your hips are too wide, your stomach sticks out, or your boobs are too small. *Shh!* You need to quiet your inner critic. Don't talk about yourself that way! If you follow all the steps we talked about—exercising, eating well, paying attention to the clothes you wear—you're not going to notice your flaws. You're only going to see your most positive attributes. Everyone has a different body type. No one shape is "better" than another—they're just different. Look around at your friends. They're probably all of varying heights and sizes. Which is a good thing—not being exactly the same as everyone else makes you special and unique.

Having a negative body image will inhibit you from finding your true inner beauty. It's important to change the dialogue you have with yourself. In the same way you need to rewrite your inner monologue about your spirituality, you need to change your inner monologue about your looks, too. Take time each day to recognize how hard you're working and give yourself some love. When you see how you look in a positive way, other people will start to see you that way as well.

Ask yourself the following questions:

> *How do I see myself? Why am I feeling that way?*
> *What do I think I ought to be seeing?*
> *How do I want others to see me?*

The answers to these questions will help you evaluate yourself and set some healthy goals. Start setting realistic goals for everything—school, sports, family, friends, your dreams, and your looks. I promise you that it will be the beginning of a beautiful, more-fulfilled, and confident future.

Remember...

GET PLENTY OF SLEEP: Getting enough zzz's is the number-one part of my beauty regimen.

NUTRITION: What goes in your body shows on the outside. Eat lots of fruits and veggies, limit your bad carb intake, and drink plenty of water.

GET MOVING: Exercise helps your mind, body, and soul—all of which contribute to true beauty.

TAKE A LITTLE EXTRA TIME: Putting extra effort into how you look goes a long way. Spending the time to style your hair, pick out the right outfit, and do your makeup will make you look and feel good!

CARE ABOUT WHAT YOU WEAR: You don't have to sport designer duds to look great. But your clothes do say something about who you are. Wear styles that enhance your body type, and steer clear of things that don't fit. Dress to impress—whether it's a potential boss or boyfriend!

LOVE YOUR LOOK: The staple of any beauty routine is how you feel about yourself. Confidence is the best outfit you could ever wear.

Now you're more than halfway along your journey toward becoming a more confident and beautiful young woman, and you're well on your way to unlocking all four keys. At this point you should be feeling, thinking, and acting like someone who knows and loves herself and is brimming with self-esteem—or at least you should know how to become that person by starting to put the keys into practice!

In Key #3 you learned how to empower yourself to become the most beautiful woman you can be. By combining what you learned in Keys #1 and #2, you can tap into that beauty from the inside out, making you one well-rounded *mujer bonita*!

If you apply what you've learned in Key #3 about nutrition and exercise, you should soon see a big difference in your physical appearance, and you should even feel different. Eating right and staying fit will enhance your mood and give you lots more energy. For me, a healthy diet keeps me feeling positive and optimistic. Changing simple things in your life, like getting to bed at a reasonable hour and substituting water for soda, can transform both your outlook and your appearance.

Continue to consult this section as needed when situations arise in your life—like when you want advice on how to wear your makeup, style your hair, or choose the right outfit for a big night out, or when you may need practical suggestions on what styles look best for your body type. You can even bring this book with you when you go shopping, so you can refer to my suggestions and use them as a guide for items you try on and purchase.

Most important, you must *feel* good about yourself in order to look your best. If I didn't have confidence in my appearance, I wouldn't be as successful as I am. Even though I know I'm not the most typically beautiful girl in the world, I know how to make myself look amazing, if I do say so myself. No one knows that back in the day I didn't know how to use an eyelash curler or apply eyeliner! I learned how to do all that girlie stuff in order to give me the knowledge I needed so I'd feel confident that I knew what I was doing—of course it was also important to have the *skills* I needed to make myself look my best. These are things that, with practice and determination, can be mastered by just about anyone.

Once I had attained the lessons from Keys #1, #2, and #3, and acquired the tools necessary to enrich my spirituality, manage my relationships with friends and family, and take control of my health and body image, I was ready to plunge into the unknown, leap into the world, spread my wings, and start making my lifelong dreams come true. Looking back I know I wouldn't have been prepared to unlock the final key unless I had followed the steps of the other keys. Now that you've come this far, it's time to unlock the final key and start turning your own aspirations into actuality.

when I decided to get back into pageants and enter Miss USA in 2003, I knew I was ready for it. I had a strong sense of who I was, with a rock-solid spiritual center. I had surrounded myself with a strong network of people who cared about me and had created relationships with them based on loyalty, commitment, and love. I had the necessary know-how for maintaining a beautiful and positive body image, I knew I had the power to take charge of my own health and looks, and I'd already achieved many of my lifelong goals—from modeling to getting a college degree (becoming only the second person in my family to do so at the time—after my big sis). The four keys had gotten me quite far, and I was excited to see how I could apply them to the next stage of my life.

I entered Miss Massachusetts USA, won the title, and went on to compete in Miss USA. I prepared for it with even more zeal than my first pageant, studying past competitions and past winners, as well as working with my coaches to get just the right look.

As the Miss USA competition whittled down, first to ten contestants, then to five, with me still in the game—I grew more and more at ease. It might sound strange, but somehow I just got really calm and comfortable. It was like the closer I got the more I could see myself winning, and that gave me a big boost of confidence. When it was time for the interview part of the contest—that's where judges ask you a question to get to know your personality, your sense of humor, your intelligence, and how quickly you can think under pressure—I was pumped. That portion can be really stressful and a lot of girls lose it during this segment. But I was having such a good time that to me it was no big deal. I told the judges about Mama Lola and her many kids, telling them, "There's girl power in my family!" And when they asked my final interview question, I had an answer. The question was "What three items would you place in a time capsule to represent the twenty-first century?" I thought about it for just a second before responding. Then I said, "I would probably have to choose a cell phone, makeup, and lastly, a computer, because the cell phone and computer tell us a lot about our century's technology and everything that has evolved since then."

That answer clinched it for me. I had gotten across my personality, and most important, my confidence. And then . . . it was time to announce the winner. This time it was my name being called out: "The winner of the Miss USA 2003 pageant is . . . Massachusetts . . . Susie Castillo!" I was being crowned Miss USA 2003! Music and streamers, cheers and tears—happy tears! By working hard, staying focused, keeping on course, and trusting in my abilities, I had made my dreams come true! I honestly believe that I'm living proof that confidence is what makes you a winner. Confidence is exactly what has made me beautiful—and what's made me succeed.

Now you've got my first three keys for attaining confidence down pat, so you're ready for the fourth and final key. This last key is the most vital step because it's the culmination of my four-part plan for unleashing your true beauty. Using everything you've learned thus far, you will now build upon the other keys with Key #4 and start turning your dreams into reality.

How do you do that?

First, you have to set goals. In this section, you'll find a foolproof goal-achieving-make-my-dreams-come-true strategy that includes figuring out what kinds of goals you wish to accomplish, creating a game plan, developing a time line, and being held accountable for your action (or nonaction). I also get you motivated with exercises designed to inspire you to stay on track and keep striving.

Certain ambitions may seem unrealistic or out of reach to many of us. I certainly felt that way at times! But often that's because we just don't know what specific steps are involved to fulfill our goals. In this section, I share the steps I took toward becoming a model, Miss USA, an actor, and who I am today. Let me tell you, there were a lot of late nights spent researching and studying on the Internet and at the library. I give you tips for how and where you can find the information you need, whether it's about finding out how to get into the college of your dreams or landing your dream job.

You'll read about how by being flexible, I was able to take my career to a whole new level by doing something I never thought I would: enter a beauty pageant. I also share with you my biggest accomplishments and give you the inside scoop on what it was like to be an MTV VJ for two and a half years.

Plus, I will guide you through exercises I use to remain focused and balanced—from journaling to positive visualization exercises to creating a personal vision board—and share tips for staying cool under pressure. These are methods you can practice whether you've got a major presentation to give, a job interview to nail, or a big event to attend—and you can even practice them in your car!

By the end of this section, you'll have a good sense of how all the keys work together and how you can apply them toward being your most positive, confident, successful, and beautiful self.

BELIEVE IN YOUR *Dreams* AND MAKE THEM A *Reality*

PHOTO BY MATTHEW LESLIE

Shooting one of my favorite shows, *Big Ten,* in South
Beach during the 2005 MTV VMAs.

Now that you've learned my first three keys for attaining true beauty, you're ready for the fourth and final key. This last key is the most important because it's the amalgamation of all the keys working together. Believing in your dreams, setting goals, and making your aspirations a reality give you the most confidence of anything you could do. Knowing I'm able to attain my goals and desires continues to be a huge ego boost to me. I've proven to myself (and those around me) that I really can achieve *anything*.

You, too, are well on your way to turning whatever your own dreams might be into reality. Want to get into art school? Become a nuclear physicist? See your name in lights? Win a Pulitzer? Be a doctor? I'm here to tell you that whatever you want for yourself, you can have it. No dream is too big or too outlandish.

Figuring It Out

Besides learning how to *look* like a model, I needed to figure out how to *become* a model. I didn't know anyone who was a model, so there was no one I could turn to for advice. I had to find out what I needed to do all on my own. But just because I didn't yet know how to become a model, I wasn't going to let that lack of knowledge stand in my way. It was just one of the hurdles I had to get over.

First, I needed to determine what information was necessary for me to know. To help, I came up with some questions.

How did models become models? Who helped them get jobs?

I learned that models used agents to get them work and that there were companies called agencies that were specifically for models.

How did I find out about agencies in my area?

I checked out the Boston Yellow Pages and looked under the heading "modeling agencies." (These days, I'd probably look online.) There were three agencies in Boston.

How did I convince them to meet with me?

I called each agency and asked the receptionists what I should do to work with their company. They all gave me the same instructions: send in a few photos of myself without too much makeup. So my older sister took some pics of me, which I submitted to the agencies with a little wish of "Please call me."

About two weeks later, I got a call back from one of the agencies. They wanted to meet with me. Whoopee! I was psyched. Both Mami and my older sister came with me to the meeting. After chatting with us for a little bit—I guess he was just trying to get to know me—the agent said he wanted to work with me. I was officially going to be represented by a modeling agency!!

My first audition was for a public-service announcement—also known as a PSA. PSAs are kind of like advertisements about things like smoking, drunk driving, and other public issues. After doing the PSA, I got lots of print work for local department stores, like Talbots. Oftentimes we'd pop open the Sunday newspaper, and there I was!! Okay, so I wasn't being featured in *Elle Magazine* or an Armani campaign, but it was a start.

Once I'd been modeling for about three years, I knew I wanted to do more, bigger, better work. Boston has a lot of great opportunities for beginning models, but the market is small beans compared to New York. Plus, I didn't want to be a print model forever. I had aspirations of being a spokesperson and actress. I didn't see that happening in Massachusetts.

One day after school, when I was hanging at a friend's house, I was flipping through a *Teen Magazine* when an ad caught my eye. It was for the *Teen* and Maybelline Cosmetics Great Model Search. Twelve finalists from around the country would be chosen to fly to Manhattan for a week of fun, photo shoots, and a final competition to determine a winner, who would be featured on the cover of *Teen*.

I knew immediately this was the kind of break I'd been looking for. I sent some photos to the contest and crossed my fingers. I'll never forget the day I came home from school to find a letter from *Teen* saying I was one of the twelve finalists! My experience in New York was amazing—I had a blast, met some great girls, learned even more about modeling, and was chosen first runner-up. That was out of about two thousand original entrants. Even though it was a huge accomplishment for me and I was pretty proud of myself, I couldn't help but feel a bit disappointed to have come so close and not win.

But my agent was thrilled and ready with a brand-new plan: he wanted me to enter the Miss Massachusetts Teen USA Pageant. He was convinced that if I was able to do so well in the *Teen*/Maybelline contest, I could probably snag top honors in the pageant. At first I couldn't believe his suggestion—to me it seemed like I would be going in an entirely different direction from what I wanted to. But he told me if I won this pageant, then went on to win other pageants, I would get the exposure I needed in order to get bigger modeling gigs and eventually become an actor. I thought about it for a while, wondering if it was the right thing for me to do. I finally decided I needed to trust my agent (after all, he had tons of experience in this industry) and be more flexible with my plan.

So that was how I got into the world of pageants. And I'm glad I did. After winning Miss USA, I went on to Miss Universe, where I placed in the top fifteen! Winning those pageants changed the course of my life. I hadn't set out to be a beauty queen, but becoming one secured the exposure and opportunities I needed to further my career and make my dreams come true—just like my agent had said it would. I'm grateful he had the foresight and belief in me, and I'm glad I had the ability to be adaptable and the insight to recognize that it was okay to alter my route.

If I Can Do It . . . You Can Do It

Think about what you want for your life. What goals would you like to achieve in your immediate future, and what goals do you want to achieve down the road? The first step in achieving any goal is acknowledging what you're passionate about and what you want to do.

Write down a list of short-term and long-term goals. When setting a goal, you want to start small and think big. By that I mean to start with a small goal first. Like maybe getting that cute guy at the coffee place to notice you. Then, no matter how small the goal is, take it seriously—"think big" about it! Entering Miss Teen Massachusetts was a small part of my overall goal, but it was a really big leap to make.

Determine What Kind of Goals You Want to Achieve

Do you want to achieve big-picture goals that will impact your future? Or do you want to accomplish smaller, more personal goals? Whether they are long-term or short-term goals, you probably have lots of different goals and want to achieve several different things at once, or maybe you want to focus on one goal at a time. It's important to know what the big picture is (your ultimate goal) so you know how best to approach it.

The most common types of goals are:

Personal. Personal goals are related to your personal development, like evolving your spirituality, volunteering, or determining what you're passionate about.

Educational. An educational goal might be getting into film school or taking a foreign-language class—anything that furthers your learning.

Creative. Do you want to paint, write, dance, or play music?

Career. Career goals could involve starting your own business or becoming a lawyer or a graphic designer.

Travel. Interested in seeing the world? Being able to travel takes major planning, as well as commitment, time, and money.

Body Image. These goals might be losing weight, getting in shape, or taking up a sport.

Relationship. What kind of relationships do you want to have in your life? Are you planning to get married someday? Do you want children?

Financial. How much money do you want to make? I'm not saying money is the most important thing. For lots of people, making just enough to cover expenses and doing what they love is fine for them. But if accumulating wealth is one of your goals, you will have to plan accordingly, by choosing a career or education path that will afford you that financial success.

Many of your aspirations might go together. For instance, your career will likely be impacted by your education. Your finances will likely be determined by your career. Creative pursuits could be related to education, career, or even personal development. Basically all these goals together can add up to big picture or lifetime achievement goals. The number of different types of goals you want to achieve may be overwhelming, but you can break them down and figure it out because it's all about what you want in your life. Remember, you can't build a house unless you first become an architect.

Creating a Game Plan

In order to achieve your goals, you need to come up with a plan, a strategy for success. Kind of like what a coach creates before a big game.

Think about the steps you need to take to reach your goal. What do you need to do in order to accomplish it? Do you need to do some research? Do you need to ask someone for advice? Maybe you need to make a few phone calls to get the right information, go to the library, or search the Internet. Write down the steps, listing them in order from what you need to do first to what you need to do last. Sometimes you might not know what you need to do last—it might come later after you've already done some of the first steps. Or you might have to break some steps down into even smaller ones.

I also think about what I need to do both physically and mentally to reach my dreams. For example, when I was competing to become Miss USA, I had to do a ton of research about the pageant, concerning what I was supposed to wear, how I was supposed to act, and what I could expect at the pageant. Researching was something I did to *mentally* help me achieve that goal. *Physically*, I ate better and went to the gym more so I would look great in my gown and swimsuit.

Set a Time Line

In order to achieve any goal, you must establish a time line and stick to it. A time line will help prevent you from procrastinating or making excuses. It also helps you track your progress. When I decided to start modeling, I gave myself a year to get signed by an agency. That meant that within that year I had to learn how to dress appropriately for the modeling industry, figure out how to wear makeup and style my hair, get in shape, and figure out which agencies to approach and schedule appointments. Dressing the part was particularly tough because I didn't exactly live somewhere where people were into high fashion, nor did I have the money to buy designer clothes, so I had to get creative. Giving myself a time limit was like insurance to me. I knew I had a clock ticking away, which made me work even harder. By the time that year was up, I'd signed with an agency.

Of course, sometimes you might miss a deadline—we all do once in a while. That's okay. Just get back on track, set a new date, and make sure you are working toward it.

 Reality Check

I don't want to dash your dreams at all, but it is important to realistically examine your abilities and limitations. You want to check that they line up with your goals. You can't be a concert pianist if you don't know how to play the piano. You can't be a pop star if you're tone deaf. There are certain dreams that might require a skill or talent that you don't have. For example, I knew I could at least try to be a model because I was tall enough. If I had been shorter, I would have changed my goals a bit. And that's okay. Sometimes we have to make adjustments to our dreams in order to achieve them.

For instance, if you really love music and want to work in the music industry, but don't have a good singing voice—there are plenty of other opportunities to work in music. You could be a producer or a DJ or a graphic designer who creates record covers.

I'm not telling you to not try—if you want to see if you can sing, go for it! But if it turns out it's not the thing for you, move on to something that suits you better. It doesn't mean you have to give up your dream altogether—it just means you're adapting it to fit you better. If you take the time to discover and develop your passion in Key #1, you'll find out pretty quickly what you're good at and what may not be quite your thing.

KEEP YOUR GOALS
in Sight

Write a list of your goals—big or small—on a sheet of paper and then tape the paper next to your bedroom door. This way you'll see your aspirations every time you leave or enter your room. Hanging the list where you can see it regularly will remind you of your goals and emphasize their significance.

JOURNALING

I like to keep a special "I Can Do It" journal in which I write down all my goals. Every morning I answer the question: What do I want to accomplish today? Then I write down my plan of action.

Every night I answer the question: What have I done to achieve my goal?

Answering this particular question makes me accountable for my actions. If I have nothing to report, I feel like I'm not working toward making my goal a reality. This is a really helpful tool in making sure I do what I say I'm going to.

Get Off the Couch

If you want to accomplish a goal, you have to actually do something about it. You can't sit around pining and wishing for something to happen—it's up to you to "make it so." You can't say, "I want to be an actress" and then hope to be discovered at your local CVS pharmacy. Sure, every once in a while, you hear stories about that happening, but it's pretty rare, like winning the lottery. So get off your couch, *sista*, and start movin'!

How do you motivate yourself? Keeping the journal helps. So does setting a schedule. Make time every day to work on your goal—whether you need to do research, study, interview someone, or practice your free throw. Whatever you need to do, spend at least an hour a day working toward your goal. I used to spend time after school every day, reading magazines, making phone calls, or practicing my techniques for applying eye shadow to get me closer to my modeling goals. Even now I spend time every day sending out headshots, setting up interviews, and checking out possible opportunities.

Even Dogs Have Goals

This is a funny story I have to share about having goals. My little dog—Lupe, the cutest Chihuahua you've ever seen (she really is—I'm not just saying that!)—loves to give me kisses on my nose. Sometimes, when she's being especially cute, I let her do it, and every once in a while, she pulls a fast one on me and gets her little tongue right up my nose! (I know—gross, right?!?) I'm totally convinced that Lupe's main goal in life is to get that little tongue as far as she can up my nose. Every single day, dozens of times a day, she balances on her back legs like a little acrobat trying to get my attention until I bring her onto my lap and let her lick my nose. That's perseverance for you! She has a goal and sticks to it. I have to say, Lupe is totally my kind of dog.

Take Risks

Taking risks can be scary. It means stepping out of your comfort zone and doing things you might find a bit daunting. But in order to achieve a goal, you will probably at some point or another have to do something you thought you wouldn't or couldn't or shouldn't.

Think of this: no successful person has become a successful person without taking some kind of risk—whether financially, physically, emotionally, or spiritually. Not Donald Trump or Cindy Crawford or Bill Gates or Beyoncé or me. We've all had to suck up our fear, hold our breath, and jump, not knowing where we'll end up. Sometimes it's important to take a leap of faith, and know that if you've prepared well, you're probably going to end up okay. And usually, taking the leap will bring you closer to your goal.

I've also found it's more satisfying to go ahead and take that risk—to try rather than not to try. Otherwise, I'll end up asking myself, "What if?" rather than, "What next?" When I decided to shoot for Miss USA, I was taking a huge risk. I had already lost one pageant—what if I lost this one, too? And what if that meant I wouldn't be any closer to my dreams? But if I *didn't* take that risk, would I be any better off? Turned out, absolutely not. It wasn't like I was getting more successful by *not* entering the pageant.

One of my favorite lyrics is from the Coldplay song "Speed of Sound" by Chris Martin: "If you never try, then you'll never know."

Be Willing to Fail

Sometimes you're going to make mistakes, you're going to mess up, you might even embarrass yourself, you will probably fail. But just like taking risks, in order to make your dreams a reality, you have to be willing to fail. Failure is an intimidating experience, and many people don't try to accomplish *anything* because they're afraid of failure. Don't give in to the fear! You actually learn, grow, and get tougher when you let yourself fail. I learned a ton about myself—my strengths, my weaknesses, and my abilities—when I lost Miss Teen USA.

Try, Try Again

The saying "If at first you don't succeed, try, try again" is totally true. If a goal is really important to you, don't give up! Keep trying again and again. If a door is slammed in your face, go knock on the next one. Try out for the team next year. Schedule an interview at another college. Send your résumé to a different firm.

One of my aspirations from when I very first started modeling was to someday be a spokesmodel. It took me thirteen years to get the Neutrogena spokesperson gig—that's a long time! But I didn't give up. I knew that eventually I would be a spokesmodel. I just had to keep trying until I landed the job.

You've Got to Work Hard

Making your dreams a reality takes a lot of work. A lot of hard, dedicated, consistent, sometimes exhausting work.

Don't expect achieving a goal to be easy. That doesn't mean it's not worthwhile, just because it's time-consuming or strenuous. You know the saying "Nothing that's worth having comes easily." Burning the midnight oil and putting in extra effort will make you appreciate what you achieve and how hard you worked. Think about those times when you were just given something without really trying. It wasn't quite as rewarding as something you put a lot of time and effort into, was it? Something you really earned.

There's a scene in the Denzel Washington movie *The Debaters* where a father tells his son, "Do what you gotta do so you can do what you wanna do." I love to think about achieving goals that way and have always lived by that rule—you have to work hard to get the payoff. Plus, I've found that working hard has definitely contributed to my true beauty by boosting my self-esteem.

Keep Your Eye on the Prize

AKA: Stay Focused. If you want to make your dreams come true, it's important to remember what you're trying to achieve. Don't go off course. Be flexible, when necessary, but don't roll totally off the track. Here are some techniques I've found helpful for remaining focused:

* Remove distractions. Distractions can be anything from your inner critic telling you that you can't achieve your goal to someone dissuading you from removing obstacles blocking your path, like time constraints, insufficient knowledge, having to learn a new skill, or being in Massachusetts instead of New York! First of all, negativity can be distracting, so you have to put on your blinders

when it comes to any kind of pessimism—either yours or others'. And as for obstacles, think of them as hurdles, part of the steps you need to take to achieve your goal. Set aside time so you can learn, practice, and find what you need in your area until you can move away if that's a necessary step for your goal.

- Prioritize. Figure out which steps are most important for achieving your goal and write them down. Start with the priorities first and do other steps later.
- Ta-da! Think about the final goal rather than obsess about the current task. The current task is a stepping-stone on the way to the end goal. Just get it done so you can move on.

Never Take No for an Answer

This has been one of the biggest lessons I've learned when going after my dreams. *I never take no for an answer.* If I have a meeting with someone, and they don't want to work with me now, I'll check back in a few months to see if they've changed their mind. Instead of hearing "no," I hear "not right now." That doesn't mean that I'm pushy or aggressive. I just choose to believe that no door is ever totally shut.

Remember my story about the time I was looking for an agent in Boston and sent photos to three agencies? At that time only one agency called me back. The others totally blew me off. Later, after I'd had some jobs, I re-sent my photos, just to see what would happen, and they *all* wanted to represent me. I didn't let those first nos stop me. I just waited until I had more experience and asked for another shot.

Ask for Help

Most people like to do things on their own and don't want to impose on other people. I've found that it's okay to ask for help. That's what friends, family, and mentors are there for. If you could help one of your friends make her dreams come true, you would, right? Most people find being asked for advice really flattering—it lets people know that you care about what they have to say. Reaching out and asking for help can put you one step (or many steps!) closer to achieving your goal. And if you've got your support system set up, you'll have plenty of people to turn to.

If no one you know can help you—find someone who can. How do you do that? Ask around—ask people in your circle. Search the Internet. Even contact your idol. That might sound intimidating, but you never know. They might love to hear from you.

I love hearing from fans! I have a MySpace page and do my best to answer every single one of my messages. Granted, sometimes it takes me forever when I'm superbusy, but I'm the only one who responds to them—I don't have an assistant or anyone doing it for me. I love helping other girls who are interested in modeling and acting, and will gladly give advice and try to help in any way I can. I'm sure there are lots of successful people out there who are willing to share their knowledge.

If you want to get in touch with someone you admire, look their name up online and see if you can find their contact information. If you can, send them an e-mail letting them know that you admire their work and would love to meet them briefly or have a short phone conversation, twenty minutes or so, to ask a few questions. You may even find a good mentor this way. Celebrities might be harder to reach, but some of them—like me—might be reachable online.

Think Positive

You are in control of your destiny. If you're going to accomplish your goals, you have to *think* that you will. We're totally in control of the messages we send ourselves.

It's really important to maintain a positive outlook, even on those days it seems like you'll never reach the finish line. If all you tell yourself is "I'm never going to make it. It's too hard. I suck," you're going to have to find a way to quiet that inner critic. If you start to think, "I can't," change your thought to "I CAN." "I quit" becomes "I'll adjust." A negative inner voice is a distraction to reaching your true potential.

Positive-Visualization Exercise

Another way to remain optimistic is by practicing positive visualization.

Whenever I have a big audition coming up, I take time out each day leading up to it to do a positive-visualization exercise. It's kind of like a meditation where I focus on the particular goal I'm shooting for.

I will sit comfortably with my eyes closed and imagine the audition.

I picture myself at the audition, imagining who I'm meeting with, what I say, and how I say it. I visualize what's said to me. I even visualize what I'm going to wear so I really feel like I'm "there."

Then I imagine myself getting the part and playing the role.

This type of visualization works well for just about any goal you're trying to reach. Have a big game coming up? Imagine your team making the winning score. Have a track meet on Saturday? Imagine yourself crossing the finish line first. Picture what the weather will be like, what you'll be wearing, how you'll feel, even what the air smells like.

If you're trying to accomplish a long-term goal, create a movie in your mind of all the steps it will take you to get there. Imagine yourself finally achieving your goal. What happens? What does it feel like?

Studies show that positive visualization actually works. It's based on the law of attraction. By visualizing, meditating on, or praying about an issue, subject, or goal, you can attract the things you want into your life. Of course, you can't just wish for something and expect it to happen without doing all the other steps. Positive visualization won't work unless it's accompanied by your hard work, dedication, and determination.

CREATE *a Vision*

OR DREAM BOARD

A great way to motivate and inspire yourself is to create a vision board: an organized collage of pictures and sayings of all the things you want to accomplish in life—no matter how big or small. Here's how you can make your own vision board.

What You'll Need
large poster board or construction paper
glue or tape
magazines

photos

mementos, like tickets, programs, flyers, etc.

affirmations (you can type your favorite sayings into a word processing
   program and then print them out)

What You'll Do

Cut out images from magazines of things that you want in life.

Cut out affirmations—words and phrases that are meaningful to
your goals.

Arrange these items on the board, without gluing.

Add photos and/or other mementos.

Organize everything on the poster board.

Then start gluing or taping.

You can also leave some spots blank, so you can add more inspiration as you find it. If you don't want to create a collage, you can use a
bulletin board instead (I like this because you can go back and rearrange, take down or add super easily).

Vision Board

One of my big goals is to be on the cover of a magazine, so I actually took
a cover of *Marie Claire*, cut out my face from a photo, and glued it on top of
the celeb who was already on the mag! I put that up on my dream board
along with a picture of a house I'd like to own one day, a list of my goals, and
a photo that I took of one of the Hollywood studios (I believe that seeing
it regularly means I will someday work there as an actor). There are also photos of my family around palm trees because I want them to move to Califor-
nia someday so we can all be closer to one another. I like to listen to a mix CD
of inspiring songs while I create my vision board. A few tunes that make me
feel like I can do anything are Israel Kamakawiwo'ole's "Somewhere over
the Rainbow," John Mayer's "Bigger Than My Body" and Hilary Duff's "Fly."

Be Flexible

You have to be willing to change the plan when necessary. Be open to new ideas, to different modes of operation. Sometimes we get so stuck in "our way" that we can't see alternatives that might actually further our progress. It's okay to restructure the plan as different opportunities or priorities arise. Embrace change when necessary!

I've had to make lots of adjustments to my strategy along the way. Funny enough, I've heard from lots of my colleagues that they've experienced this, too. It's common, so anticipate the likelihood that you will experience some shifts here and there, but don't let the changes distract you. Stay focused on the ultimate goal.

In 2005 I became a VJ on MTV hosting shows like *Total Request Live*, *MTV's Spring Break*, *Backstage at the VMAs*, *Big Ten*, and *The Real World Reunion Specials*. Working as one of only five MTV VJs was an amazing opportunity. At one point there were actually just two of us, and I remember sitting in the makeup room getting ready to host *TRL* and thinking, "Wow, this is insane! I'm an MTV VJ!" I met and interviewed some of the world's biggest celebrities, like Tom Cruise, Jessica Alba, Will Ferrell, Shakira, and Jennifer Lopez.

However, working at MTV wasn't the kind of job I was pursuing after my reign as Miss USA ended. At the time, I had just moved to Los Angeles to begin my career in acting, which had been my goal before I won Miss USA. Being an MTV VJ was not part of my plan.

So when I was offered the gig, I had some hesitation, but then thought, "How can I pass up such an amazing opportunity?" The answer was: I couldn't! This was an unexpected door that had opened in my life, and I figured it could be another stepping-stone, like Miss USA was. I took the job, which opened the door to many other opportunities.

In addition to my on-camera hosting duties, MTV gave me another job hosting a radio show for them called *TR-Latino*. I was also hired often to host events across the country, like the New York City launch of the Nintendo Wii. But one of the most amazing opportunities happened at the 2006 MTV Movie Awards, when I met the president of one of MTV's biggest sponsors, Neutrogena. Soon after, I became a spokesperson for them! During that time I also landed my first movie role, playing Diana Flores in Disney's *Underdog*. I got the part without even having to audition—all because of my performance and exposure on MTV. I was soon blessed with yet more opportunities: hosting the live telecast of the 2005 Miss Teen USA Pageant, and shortly after leaving MTV, I was hired to host another show, *America's Prom Queen,* for ABC Family. ABC saw my work on MTV and thought that I would be perfect to host their show, which turned out to be one of the best hosting jobs I've ever had.

Aside from working with an amazing crew at MTV and learning a ton about production, the biggest lesson that I learned from my MTV experience was that I shouldn't be afraid to alter my life plan when opportunities come knocking on my door. One opportunity could lead to another and then to another. You just never know where life is going to take you, so make sure you're open to change and welcome it.

Accountability

Accountability is kind of like taking inventory, or stock, of the progress you make toward achieving your goal. You probably already know about being accountable. Usually accountability comes with either a reward or a consequence. You've likely dealt with these kinds of situations in your own life: you have to show up for a job or you might get fired; you have to turn in homework or you might fail a course. If you do these things, you're likely to get a pay-check (reward) or an A on your report card. When you're striving to make your dreams a reality, it's necessary that you are accountable to yourself. After all, these goals and dreams are about you.

One way to measure accountability is to create a series of milestones, or deadlines, for yourself. Deadlines are great for motivating you to get something done. When I started modeling, I knew that before I turned fifteen I wanted to be signed with an agency. So every month I had a log of things I had to accomplish in order to make that deadline.

Keeping track of all the things I did along the way really helped me see exactly what I was doing and where I was go-ing. I wrote lists of steps I needed to take in my journal and then checked them off as I accomplished each one. Seeing the checkmarks was really exciting—I could literally see I was getting closer to my goal.

You can also keep track of your accountability by creat-ing a support team. Let your friends and family know what you're trying to accomplish, and ask if you can check in with them regularly about your progress. Mami and I had daily conversations about what I was doing, what I'd done, and what I still needed to do. I still call her just about every single day for our check-ins. They're incred-ibly helpful and keep me balanced and focused. Plus, I feel even better knowing I have her behind-the-scenes support!

Healthy Competition

I love to be challenged, so I find competing a lot of fun. That's why I was so in to sports, and it's probably why I picked such a competitive career. There's something about competition that gets me pumped up and makes me strive harder. Of course, there are a few things I have to keep in mind—you should, too:

* Be prepared. This is crucial! You can't expect to win a marathon by learning to run on race day. You need to study and practice long before you get to the course.
* Enjoy the journey. Part of reaching a goal is the journey you take to get there. If you don't take time to recognize and appreciate the steps it takes to get you to your destination, you won't appreciate the end result as much. Have fun playing the game!
* Be a gracious loser. If you lose, don't throw a tantrum or be rude. Sure, it's frustrating—even devastating—that you didn't win, but think about everything you learned along the way. Think of how much fun you had in your journey. And remember, there's always another opportunity for you out there.
* Be a gracious winner. Congratulations! You won! Be humble and polite about your success. Being haughty or conceited is just plain rude. Plus, it makes you look bad.

Reward Yourself

When you've worked so hard, it's important to reward your-self for a job well done. At each milestone, give yourself a treat—whether it's a spa night with the girls, renting your favorite movie, or just taking a day to do nothing. Giving ourselves rewards rejuvenates us and keeps us motivated to keep going. Here are some ways I've rewarded myself over the years:

- When my volleyball team would win a big game, we would have pasta nights or go out to one of our favorite restaurants to celebrate.
- When I won Miss Massachusetts USA, I threw a fun fund-raising party for a charity and to help my family attend the Miss USA Pageant in San Antonio, Texas, that year.
- When I signed my VJ contract with MTV, I went to the Gucci store on Rodeo Drive in Beverly Hills and bought myself a cute little bag I had seen on *Sex and the City*! What a splurge!

Staying Cool Under Pressure

OMG! You got an interview at that fabulous new boutique. Your stomach's in knots because you want the job so bad, but you want to make a good impression. When I'm excited about an audition, interview, or event, I have a few techniques to keep from blowing my top.

TAKE A DEEP BREATH IN . . . AND OUT. . . .

Breathing is the best way to soothe stress.

Try to find a quiet space.

Close your eyes.

Inhale a long, deep breath.

Hold it for one count.

Exhale long and deep.

Hold the exhale at the bottom of the breath for one count.

Repeat this between five to ten times.

This breathing exercise should slow your heart rate and make you feel more calm. It's a great technique to use before any event that might make you anxious. And remember: you're not anxious or nervous—you're excited (wink)!

EAT

Make sure you've had something to eat before an event. You don't want to be distracted by hunger or a growling stomach. Just don't eat anything too heavy—you don't want to feel too full or have a stomachache. If I don't want to eat a full meal, I will usually have a small salad with extra-virgin olive oil, white balsamic vinegar, sea salt, pepper, and sometimes avocado.

DO-RE-MI

This might sound a little silly, but humming or singing a song helps relieve tension for me. On my way to an audition, it's like *American Idol* in the car. I'm belting out my favorite songs. When I'm in a public place, I turn down the volume a bit to a low hum. Humming soothes nerves and takes your mind off your worries.

WORK IT OFF

If you have time to go for a run, take a yoga class, or do some stretches before the event, exercise is a helpful way to destress. Plus, working out releases endorphins, which make us feel happier and more relaxed. Try skipping rope or doing some jumping jacks if you don't have time for a full-on workout.

I Know I Can. I Know You Can.

I was the third Latina to be crowned Miss USA—just the third! That in itself is so incredible to me because winning Miss USA became much more than a stepping-stone for my career. It was an opportunity for me to continue doing community service, but on a national level. I instantly became a spokesperson for breast and ovarian cancer, and also traveled the United States and even Korea with the USO (the United Service Organization). Winning the crown was also an opportunity for me to break the stereotypes about both Latinos *and* pageant girls.

In 2003, just after I'd won Miss USA, I made *People en Español*'s "Most Beautiful" list. When I found out, I was thrilled! It was such a compliment to be honored among some of my favorite Latin musicians and actors. But even more important than being awarded that designation was the personal confirmation that I was on the right track, that I knew exactly what I was doing, and that my intuition about what worked best for me actually did—despite the naysayers, who had said I wouldn't, shouldn't, couldn't even become a model or compete in the pageants. I have to admit that part of me wanted to autograph that magazine and send it to the uncle who said I wouldn't win Miss Massachusetts USA.

It doesn't matter where you come from, what your home life is like, whether your hair is black or blond, your skin light or dark—you can achieve more than you've probably ever thought possible. So dare to dream, homie! Think big, set goals, work hard, and reach for the stars.

Remember...

SET GOALS: Making your dreams a reality is all about setting and achieving goals. Start with small goals and then work up to bigger aspirations.

FIGURE IT OUT: If you don't know how to achieve your goal, do some research. Look up stuff on the Internet, go to the library, and ask people.

MAKE IT HAPPEN: Don't just talk about it—do it.

CREATE A PLAN: Come up with a step-by-step plan that includes both long- and short-term goals, milestones, and a time line.

TAKE RISKS: Step out of your comfort zone.

BE WILLING TO FAIL: Making mistakes is part of the journey.

TRY, TRY AGAIN: Keep trying and don't give up.

WORK HARD: Be prepared to put in long hours and use lots of elbow grease.

KEEP YOUR EYE ON THE PRIZE: Stay focused on your goal.

DON'T TAKE NO FOR AN ANSWER: If someone says no, try again at a later time. You'll be more experienced, and the person you're asking just might have a need for you.

ASK FOR HELP: We can't do everything on our own. Ask for help, whether it's information, mentoring, tutoring, or actual physical help.

BE FLEXIBLE: Be willing (and ready) for your plans and goals to change.

THINK POSITIVE: Have an optimistic outlook.

BE ACCOUNTABLE: Keep track of your progress and check off steps as you complete them. Use a journal or a friend to help.

REWARD YOURSELF: Be sure to recognize your accomplishments with treats, which could be anything from new shoes to a night out to a day in bed!

Key #4 is the last step toward realizing your true potential. It's the pinnacle of the *Confidence Is Queen* life philosophy. As you can see, turning your dreams into reality is definitely possible. If you follow the guidelines I presented in Key #4, you should be able to achieve just about anything you decide to attempt—just like I did! All you have to do is make a choice, have patience, and go for it.

You can start practicing these principles right away and use them as you set your own personal, creative, or big-picture goals. Whenever I embark on a new goal, I write down what I hope to accomplish and refer to it every single day. This ensures that I stay focused on my journey. I encourage you to do the same. It's also important to create a detailed plan so you have a guide to follow and you know exactly what steps you need to accomplish to get closer to your big goal. Refer back to this section when you need a refresher on how to design a game plan. Just as important is establishing a time line to ensure you get things done. I love to set deadlines for myself—it keeps me challenged. Plus, if I meet a milestone, I treat myself, whether it's dinner at my favorite restaurant, a new pair of shoes, or sleeping in. Those little rewards make all the hard work worth it—and I have the knowledge that I'm *that much closer* to accomplishing my goal, which is a reward in itself.

Sure, making your dreams come true takes work, but here's the thing: that dedication is all about improving yourself, making yourself a better person, making your life better, being happy, and giving yourself opportunities and possibilities that you didn't have before. Plus, hard work equals pride, which equals confidence, which equals beauty.

As your life progresses, your aspirations will likely change, too. That's normal. My goals are constantly morphing and adapting. That's why it's important to remain flexible and be open to all possibilities as they come your way! You never know what unexpected break might lead you in a whole new direction. I find life really exciting in that regard. I don't know what my job is going to be at the end of the year but I'm constantly surprising myself with my capabilities so I'm confident that it will be something amazing.

Keep in mind as you practice the keys in your own life that all of them—from Key #1 to Key #4—are interdependent and work best when used together. For example, when you're working toward a goal, it's important to limit negative distractions, especially if they're coming from you. One way to do that is to call on what you learned in Key #1 about how to quiet your inner critic. Another example is when you encounter a road block and need help with something, you should feel free to call on the support network you learned how to build in Key #2 to assist you. All of the guidelines I've presented in this book can work together, and often work even *better* when used together.

PHOTO BY MATTHEW LESLIE

My beautiful sisters, Yaralia (*left*) and Marisele (*right*), at an event in Boston with me. I love when I can share my experiences with my family.

Well, we've reached the end of our journey together. By this point you should have a deeper understanding
of how I got where I am today and recognize that my success,
sense of beauty, and even happiness have been contingent
upon one thing: confidence. Without confidence, I'd still be
that girl in Methuen, Massachusetts, and my life would have
turned out completely differently. Not that the life I would
have had otherwise would have been bad by any means, but it
wasn't the life that I wanted for myself. Had I stayed there, I
may have been unhappy and regretful of not trying to live out
my dreams—and who wants to live with regret!?

Look around you and think about who you know who
exemplifies inner strength and self-assurance. Maybe it's
someone close to you, a coworker at your job, or even a celebrity. Keep in mind that they likely weren't born with all that
certainty. They probably had to learn it and then practice it
regularly, just like I do—and just like you will, too.

Someone who I find incredibly inspiring both spiritually

and professionally is Oprah Winfrey. Now, you may be saying, "Well, duh! Who doesn't look up to Oprah?" Exactly! To me, she's someone who really personifies many of the principles of my four keys. Oprah is not only the most successful television personality in the world, but she's also an incredible humanitarian who is always giving what she can in order to make the world a better place for those who are underprivileged. She definitely has a spirit that reminds me of what Mama Lola was talking about when she used to tell me: "There are always people in the world who are in need, and we must do what we can for them." Oprah does just that!

Not to mention that Oprah has overcome some of the most difficult life circumstances imaginable. But she had the courage and confidence to overcome those obstacles.

Like Oprah, I know that my own journey of personal growth is far from over. There are many goals I have yet to accomplish. I'm still working on becoming a full-time actor. Sure, I've gotten a few acting roles, but I want to play bigger parts that will allow my talent and skill to grow. Someday I want to star in my own sitcom. That's my biggest professional dream!

Of course, I have other dreams, too. Following in Oprah's footsteps, I want to use my celebrity to continue to give to those less fortunate and champion causes that are important to me. I also want to continue getting out my message of hope to kids who might be feeling lost and hopeless, as well as inspiring young women—especially Latinas—that they don't have to succumb to society's stereotypes of them. I want to make sure they know they have options and encourage them to look for opportunities.

I have personal goals I wish to accomplish, as well. It's important to me to maintain spiritual balance in my life and to nurture my relationships with family, friends, and especially my husband. In addition, I want to continue being healthy, fit, and beautiful, inside and out. One of my biggest dreams has always been to help my mother retire early. I want to support her just as she supported us. Mami loves gardening, so one day I plan to buy her a beautiful house with a sunny yard so she can create her dream garden.

In order to accomplish all of these desires, I will continue to draw on the four keys as they apply to each particular situation I face, from going to auditions to hanging out with my sisters or getting ready for red-carpet events. I find that as my life and career have progressed, and as I've gained more knowledge and experience, the keys have become an even more valuable and integral part of my overall life strategy. I still turn to them, even now that I'm an adult and married. In fact, I use them more now than ever. Because I've relied on the keys to get me to this point in accomplishing both my personal and professional aspirations I know that I will continue to rely on them far into my future and, likely, forever. They are timeless!

Each day brings forth a new challenge, but I don't spend time getting anxious or worrying about it because I know I've got the keys to guide me through whatever test or obstacle might arise. Every morning when I wake up, I repeat my inner monologue to myself, "I am beautiful. Treat people the way you want to be treated." And if I'm going to an audition or a job interview that day I tell myself: "I am going to blow them away and get this job!"

Communication is *muy importante* in every facet of life. Although difficult at times, I continue to speak up when I want to be heard, set boundaries when necessary, and try to always treat people with dignity, respect, love, and (if work-related) an air of professionalism, all lessons that stem from Key #2.

After positive self-talk, I head to the kitchen and whip up the Green Lemonade that I gave you the recipe for in Key #3. Everything I recommended you eat in Key #3, I eat every day. I plan to practice the rules of good health and nutrition for the rest of my life because eating right makes me feel awesome and look amazing! You really are what you eat, so when I'm eighty-five years old, I plan to be sharp as a tack and still playing volleyball.

If I have a big event coming up, and I'm unsure about what to wear or how to style my hair, I do research—just like I did back in the days when I was preparing to compete in beauty pageants. I get the latest fashion magazines, find out what's on this season's runway, and ask questions of people who know that sort of thing, like the stylists that I work with on different television projects. Key #3 reminds me that taking just a little extra time to prepare will definitely show in the final result!

To prepare for a big meeting that I'm really nervous about, I'll practice the positive-visualization exercises in Key #4 to stay calm and focused. Taking time out to breathe, relax, and envision a successful outcome definitely helps me stay positive, optimistic, and confident.

As you can see, I use elements from all four keys regularly in my daily life. They all work together, fitting with one another like pieces of a puzzle. For example, if I landed a role in a big movie, I'd probably call on Key #1 to give me strength, Key #2 to remind me how to interact with my coactors, Key #3 to ensure I look my best, and Key #4 to keep me on track for making my dreams come true.

Now that I've shared with you the route I took to become the Susie Castillo who won Miss USA, became an actor, a VJ on MTV, a spokesperson for Neutrogena, and wrote this book, you should be well equipped to become the most beautiful, successful, and confident individual you can be! You can take the lessons I learned and put them to practice in your own life. I'm sure that soon the keys will become an integrated part of your life plan.

Many of the philosophies I've presented in this book aren't new or revolutionary, but I think my approach to them is definitely fresh and unique. I think most young women can relate to my story: feeling like an outsider, feeling like a stereotype, and even feeling hopeless when we have longings for who we want to be and what we want to achieve that seem totally out of reach.

By following these keys both you and I will be able to attain everything we've ever wanted, whether it's to be beautiful or creative or smart or funny or wealthy. I believe that we attract certain things to our lives, both good and bad, and I believe we possess the power to turn negative aspects into positive ones. It's like the yin-yang principle—there's positive in the negative and negative in the positive. However, it's when you're experiencing something negative that you must focus on what's positive in the situation. That's when you gain enough inner strength to overcome and persevere.

One of the beliefs I hold most dear is that every woman deserves to be beautiful and can be beautiful in her own way. Beauty is important because it makes us feel special, powerful, happy, and content. It's about becoming the best person you can possibly be: spiritually, personally, physically, creatively, professionally. It's a lifelong process that needs to be worked on every single day, so don't beat yourself up if you don't see a change immediately. I promise you will see progress, though, if you stick to the keys and are patient, loving, and gentle to yourself. Remember, I first started working in the entertainment industry as a model when I was fourteen years old, and it wasn't until 2003, when I won

Miss USA, that I got my "big break." I worked hard for almost a decade!

Of course, I have times that get me down—don't we all?!?

Sometimes, professionally, things don't go my way. I go to lots of auditions for parts I don't end up getting. Those events certainly make it difficult to keep my confidence level up, especially when I've been rejected for a job I really, really wanted. Or a character I really connected with and thought I was perfect for. Rejection sucks, but I know it's a hazard of the entertainment business. In fact, rejection is a part of life. During these times, I remind myself that it's the one part I do get that matters. That's the one I want—and that's what keeps me going, ready to try out for the next part.

Other times, my relationships get off-kilter, and I just can't seem to communicate with anyone. Or I wake up with a big pimple on my nose. Or I just feel totally blah. No one's perfect all the time. Sometimes we need the bad times in order to remind us how great the good times are. They give us a reality check and energize us to keep on keeping on.

As you grow older and gain more experience, you'll find that you can apply the four keys to just about every stage of your life, from moving out on your own to building your career to getting married and starting a family. They will also guide you no matter what path you take, whether your goal is to become a world traveler, go to film school, or head your own company. It's like a personal GPS navigation system!

Over the next few years, I plan to achieve my goal of becoming an actor. Don't be surprised if you see me on a TV show playing one of the leads! I hope that you'll be there to watch me (and cheer me on!).

I want you to know that I'll be cheering you on, too, and hope that, as you set out on your own personal journey, the four keys will help you unlock the door to all of life's wonderful blessings and everything you desire: love, happiness, beauty, and most of all, confidence.

XOXO,
Susie

RE YOUR *relationships* DEVELOP YOUR *spirituality* TAKE CONTRO

lth BELIEVE IN YOUR *dreams* NURTURE YOUR *relationships* DEV

rituality TAKE CONTROL OF YOUR *health* BELIEVE IN YOUR *dreams*

elationships DEVELOP YOUR *spirituality* TAKE CONTROL OF YOUR h

E IN YOUR *dreams* NURTURE YOUR *relationships* DEVELOP YOUR spi

y TAKE CONTROL OF YOUR *health* BELIEVE IN YOUR *dreams* NURTURE YOUR

ships DEVELOP YOUR *spirituality* TAKE CONTROL OF YOUR *health*

reams NURTURE YOUR *relationships* DEVELOP YOUR spiritua

L OF YOUR *health* BELIEVE IN YOUR *dreams* NURTURE YOUR relatio

P YOUR *spirituality* TAKE CONTROL OF YOUR *health* BELIEVE IN YOUR d

RE YOUR *relationships* DEVELOP YOUR *spirituality* TAKE CONTR

ACKNOWLEDGMENTS

First and foremost I thank God for all the blessings that He continues to bestow upon me and for giving me the strength to overcome my challenges. A million thank-yous to *mi querida madre*, whose strength and undying support inspired me to write this book. My husband and gift, Matt, for his love, support in all that I do, and his beautiful laughter. Big thanks to my best friends and sisters, Marisele and Yaralia, for being wonderful cheerleaders and caring siblings. A special thanks to Sue and Steve Leslie for raising a fine young man who brings me joy every day and for their unconditional support. I would also like to acknowledge Ray Garcia and Kerry Donovan for all of their help, patience, and hard work in this process. Big "xoxo" to Scott Buchheit and Phil Mucci for lending a helping hand when it was much needed. The cover is da bomb digity! Lastly, a special thank-you to Apryl Lundsten for helping me realize the dream that you are holding in your hands.